DIE YOUNG...
As late as possible

Herb Kavet

2 2 November 2008

PENTAGON PRESS

Die Young ... As late as possible

Published by Boston America Corp.
325 New Boston Street
Woburn, Massachusetts 01801

Indian edition published by
PENTAGON PRESS
206, Peacock Lane, Shahpur Jat, New Delhi-110049
Phones : 011-64706243, 26491568
Telefax : 011-26490600
www.pentagon-press.com
email : rajan@pentagon-press.com

ISBN : 978-81-8274-356-4

Printed by
Ritomate International
Noida Special Economic Zone, India.
www.ritomate.com

*Interior page design and composition
by Stephen Tiano,
Book Designer, Page Compositor and Layout Artist*

1 3 5 7 9 10 8 6 4 2

Table of Contents

3 CORE   51

Acknowledgments

MY POOR, PATIENT WIFE read each chapter, made suggestions, and diligently corrected the grammar and spelling. (She did win every grammar award in high school.) Bored to tears as I resubmitted each chapter she also stoically listened to my endless discussions of nutrition. Son Gregg, a real Hollywood writer, admonished me to "punch it up" and while I still don't quite know what that means his suggestions probably shortened the book by half. Younger son Matt, usually loves everything I write, but couldn't make it through the Nutrition chapter so I reworked it. The reader will be happy that it was simplified. Friend and neighbor Gene Tremblay took many of the photos and the idea of making your life curve more rectangular was stolen from him.

Thanks to Mark Dabagian who completed the cartoons in record time. Stephen Tiano did an impeccable job of designing and laying out the book, and the cover (which perhaps made you buy the book) was designed by Kim Williamson. Printing was by my good friend Rajan of Pentagon Press in New Delhi, India. Justin Cash (www.justincash.com) did the cover photography and made me look better than I ever hoped.

Herb Kavet
Wayland, MA 01778
hkavet@comcast.net

Acknowledgments viii

In the bottle before you is a pill, a marvel of modern medicine that will regulate gene transcription throughout your body, helping prevent heart disease, stroke, diabetes, obesity, and 12 kinds of cancer—plus gallstones and diverticulitis. Expect the pill to improve your strength and balance as well as your blood lipid profile. Your bones will become stronger. You'll grow new capillaries in your heart, your skeletal muscles, and your brain, improving blood flow and the delivery of oxygen and nutrients. Your attention span will increase. If you have arthritis, your symptoms will improve. The pill will help you regulate your appetite and you'll probably find you prefer healthier foods. You'll feel better, younger even, and you will test younger according to a variety of physiologic measures. Your blood volume will increase, and you'll burn fats better. Even your immune system will be stimulated. There is just one catch.

There's no such pill. The prescription is exercise.

EPIGRAPH TEXT REPRINTED WITH PERMISSION
FROM "THE DEADLIEST SIN," BY JONATHAN SHAW,
FIRST PUBLISHED IN THE MARCH–APRIL 2004 ISSUE
OF *HARVARD MAGAZINE.*
COPYRIGHT © 2004 HARVARD MAGAZINE INC.
ALL RIGHTS RESERVED.

Introduction

SOME YEARS AGO I was skiing in Vermont and saw an old guy with a 10th Mountain Division badge on his ski. The 10th was an elite mountain division created at the beginning of World War ll by the leading skiers in the country. After the war this legendary group sparked the U.S. skiing boom. I knew some guys in the 10th from my army service and maneuvered through the lift line to share memories with this fellow and perhaps take a few runs. Now I'm not a bad skier. I've spent my ski life keeping up with my sons who were top college racers and I don't take rest stops. But this guy, who had to be at least 80, easily beat me down and was waiting for me at the bottom. When I commented on his skiing skills he talked about aging. He said with an old Vermonter's drawl, "You know there are three things that keep you young." And I was

listening very intently because he had obviously found the secret of staying young. "Before anything", he said, "you gotta have good genes. Then, you have to be athletic, you have to be optimistic and you have to be heroic." At that moment we got off the lift and he skied away. I've spent years pondering just what this old fellow meant. This book is what I've figured out.

My Credentials

I'm not an M.D. I don't even have a PhD in sport physiology. I went to M.I.T. so maybe I'm smart but I still have to call my wife for help whenever I try something new on my computer. As a kid I was among the least athletic in all of Brooklyn. Schoolmates would fight to get me *off* their teams. My high school athletics consisted of the Photo and Spanish Clubs. In college I stayed on the freshman swim team for about a day.

When I entered the army I volunteered for airborne training. You do lots of running at jump school and when I got married I continued to exercise. In my late 30's I took up fencing, something that had always fascinated me. I practiced diligently and in a few years was qualifying for the Nationals (no big deal) and actually taking home gold medals in my age group (also no big deal as by this time there was practically no one in my age group). Once I did manage to reach the top 10 in a "B" category.

At the time I belonged to a health club where I would play tennis, swim and lift weights. One day a staff member bugged me to enter the club triathlon. I had no interest in this silly sport but finally signed up just to get him to stop bothering me. To my surprise I won. Not my age group, mind you, and not the B level. I won the whole damn thing. While I wasn't a great swimmer and only biked recreationally and didn't particularly like running I was okay at all of them. That evidently was enough in this new discipline. I had found my sport. In 1982 at age 45, I started training seriously, hired a coach and over the next 10 years raced almost every summer weekend. I completed over 70 triathlons and won enough age group trophies to clutter the house. In 1989 I qualified for the U.S. team at the World Championship in Avignon, France.

Some years later while competing in New Hampshire a couple of bearded bums in a pickup truck cursed at me and tried to run me off the road. I was feeling quite vulnerable at the time biking along in my little Speedo with no other competitors in sight. I wanted to yell "stop and fight" but knew they would beat me to a pulp should they take up the challenge. I was determined not to let that happen again. The next week I started boxing lessons.

Boxing led to years of karate and black belts and finally Brazilian Jiu Jitsu. My business partner, tiring of hearing descriptions of my latest moves once remarked in exasperation, "Herb, at your age you're not going to get into a fight." He was right, but the value of the martial arts wasn't tackling some bully in a bar. It was the confidence and youthful feeling it

gave me. How could you not feel good when sparring with kids 40 and 50 years younger than yourself.

Around this time I retired from serious triathlon competition. While I still swam, biked and ran, the martial arts evidently fulfilled all of my psychological athletic needs. Something else came with this fitness and confidence. People couldn't believe I was 70. Looking at other 70 year olds made me think I was doing something very right. Perhaps I had a story to tell.

A Lifestyle for Staying Young

This book is going to give you a program or, more accurately, a life-style philosophy for staying young. You can get exercise and nutrition advice from hundreds of books. This book ties together exercise, nutrition and, most importantly, a positive mental attitude to allow you to stay young as long as possible.

There are six components to staying fit. You need to exercise your aerobic system, your muscle structure, your core; maintain flexibility through stretching; and eat healthy. At the same time you've got to think, act and feel like a young person. Following these ideas will enable you to continue a youthful lifestyle years beyond what most people consider doddering old age.

"Know Thyself"

The ancient Greeks had two key philosophical concepts engraved on the great Shrine at Delphi. The first was "Know Thyself". It's hard to stay young if you're constantly lying to yourself about your weight, your exercise intensity, your attitudes and your diet. It's difficult to truly "Know Thyself" but start by taking a good look at yourself and evaluating your body and your mental state.

What should you evaluate?

1. The best measure of your aerobic fitness is how quickly your heart recovers after vigorous exercise. The healthier your heart, the quicker it will recover after exercise. Put simply, if your heart rate drops 50 beats one minute after vigorous exercise, you are in excellent condition. If it drops only 20 beats you are in

"Know Thyself"

very average condition. Less than that you are in poor condition.

2. Look in a mirror while undressed. Try to look honestly so you can see what you look like and not what you imagine yourself to look like. Take a photo in a bathing suit. Photos don't lie as much as mirrors do. How is your muscle tone?

3. What hurts? If your back is giving you problems it's likely your core is weak. Other constant aches and pains point up problem areas. Some can be cured by exercise and some may need medical attention.

4. How much weight have you gained since college? I can still wear my old army uniform from my paratrooper days, 50 years ago. Can you still fit into a very old pair of pants?

5. How's your diet? Are you eating donuts and saturated fat or have you learned about whole grains and vegetables?

6. Can you still "think young"? If you've ever said "Oh, I'm too old for that" or "I don't do that anymore" your mental state needs some work.

Nothing in Excess

The second engraving at Delphi was "Nothing in excess". This is another key that I'm interpreting to mean no single activity or discipline should be done to excess. It's hard to stay young by doing one thing, no matter how much or how good you are at it. You may bike centuries each weekend or run 15 miles a day or spend hours lifting weights or do yoga till you can tie yourself in knots or eat an organic vegan diet. And as you complete one of these activities you may feel like you are doing a fine job of staying young. But you are not. All these things are great by themselves. Individually they won't keep you young. You've got to do them all. Exercise aerobically or you are likely to have heart and weight problems. Lift weights or your bones and upper body will deteriorate. Work your core or you'll have back and digestive problems. Ignore stretching and your range of motion will diminish and affect all your other activities. Eat junk and all the exercise in the world will not save you from disease and lack of energy. Your diet may be perfect

Nothing in Excess

but without exercise your muscles will slacken, belly sag and your cardio-vascular system with‹ idea is not to concentrate your physical efforts ‹ direction. *Nothing in excess.* Eat properly, get i‹ aerobic activity, lift some weights, stretch and ‹ on your core. Keep varying your workouts and ‹ skip any of the components and you'll stay young much longer.

The Whole Story

This introductory chapter actually tells the whole, if abbreviated, story. To stay young you have to do some sort of regular and stimulating aerobic exercise. And you probably should be doing it 3 to 5 times a week. Running, swimming, biking, rowing, cross-country skiing and many other activities that get you breathing hard are the key to your cardio-vascular health and probably the biggest life extending activity you can do. Add to this some resistance training, such as weight lifting, a few times a week. This not only makes you look better at the beach but also prevents all sorts of injuries. Your upper body goes to hell after age 50 unless you stress the muscles. If you don't use a particular muscle for 30 or 40 years it stands to reason that muscle is going to atrophy. It's the old "use it or lose it" concept.

As you get older stretching becomes more important. Want to avoid being hunched over or walking with a shuffle as you age? Try stretching every day. Better yet join a yoga group so you'll get some feedback and instruction.

Your core is the muscle in your middle and these muscles hold the whole body together. To avoid back problems, posture deterioration, and to keep a flat abdomen you have to exercise your core. The "six pack" abs you see in the underwear ads do more than look good. They and other more critical core muscles hold your spine in place and prevent back problems. A strong core also contributes mightily to an efficient digestive system.

While you have to do the physical part, the most important aspect of staying young may be your mental attitude. If you remember reading in the beginning of this chapter (and if you're not so old that you've already forgotten) I mentioned the old 10th Mountain Division skier who said youth was a matter of being athletic, optimistic and heroic. Being optimistic is having a positive and happy mental attitude and I like to associate heroic with the concept of a youthful and exciting life style. That'll keep you from aging. If you continue to do heroic things: sports and activities with your children or younger people, new things, daring things, even idiotic somewhat dangerous things you will keep a young and positive outlook and avoid falling into the devastating "Oh I'm too old for that" state of mind. Once you feel you're too old to do something you will find you ARE too old to do it and it is a downward spiral after that.

The final concept is eating healthy. Yes, I know the guidelines of what is healthy and what is deadly seem to change with each newspaper article. But if you do some reading on your own, keep aware of the latest suggestions made by government agencies and

Acting heroic helps keep you young

leading medical authorities, you will focus in on the best current theory. Eat whole grains, legumes, non-fat dairy products and lots of fruits and vegetables. Try smaller portions of lean meat, chicken and fish. Avoid animal fats, sugar, simple carbohydrates and anything highly processed and you can't go far wrong.

1 The Aerobics of Life

Ｉf you have to pick one concept from this book to follow let it be this one. *Aerobics.* Aerobics is a word coined by Dr. Kenneth Cooper in his landmark book *Aerobics* in 1968. Aerobics describes exercise that stimulates your cardio-vascular system through vigorous sustained effort. It is probably the single most important thing that will extend your life and keep you young. In an extensive study published in the prestigious *Journal of the American Medical Association* in 1989, and many others since then, unfit men were over 3 times as likely to die from all causes as fit men.

Jonathan Shaw said it all in the quote from the Harvard Magazine at the beginning of this book. *The magic pill, the marvel of modern medicine that will improve all aspects of your health is exercise.* He's talking about aerobic exercise. Resistance or weight training, stretching, sports, and core fitness all have their place, but aerobic activity is the one that will give you the biggest return.

Aerobics are any activity that will get your heart beating at a faster rate and your lungs pumping harder than when they are at rest. Running, biking, swimming, rowing, cross country skiing and various group aerobic sessions come to mind first, but actually anything that gets your heart rate up and stresses your breathing will work. Yes, sex can be considered an aerobic activity too though it takes an awful lot of it to really do much good. The key is to stress your aerobic system, your heart and lungs, at a serious intensity and for a serious length of time. Moderately vigorous gardening, for example, can be an aerobic exercise but it's hard to measure and less efficient than jogging or biking.

There are many theories of how much and how intense the aerobic activity has to be to provide benefits. I've seen articles claiming yard work or housework provides adequate amounts and I've seen endless people gently floating in a pool, perhaps swimming a length or walking slowly around their neighborhood as they carry on a casual conversation. They consider this perfectly sufficient aerobic exercise. Don't believe it. I belong more to the "no pain no gain" school. Moderate exercise, of course, is better than nothing at all but if you're really interested in staying young until you die it's lots better to push yourself with something that requires effort and a little sweat. One simple measure of effort is whether you can carry on a comfortable conversation while you perform the exercise. If you can easily and continuously talk while you're jogging or biking, you're probably not working as hard as you should. And it is vastly better for your aerobic conditioning to work out intensely a few times a week than to do something very easy every day.

Intensity and Rest

When I first started doing triathlons I had a coach. Patti Cashman was a national bike time trial champion, a junior Olympic swimmer and Olympic level rower. She really knew her stuff. At the time I was running one mile every day. Patti informed me, in no uncertain terms, that this was bringing me practically no benefit. "It's better to run 3 miles, a few times a week, rather than a mile every day" she said, introducing me to the idea of *INTENSITY & REST.*

Kenyan runners learn intensity is the key to aerobic conditioning

Intensity and rest is probably the most important concept in fitness. When a muscle (or organ) is stressed, micro tears appear in its fibers. To increase the strength of the muscle these tears must be given a chance to heal. That's why intensity and then rest is so important. First you have to stress or tear the micro fibers of the muscle and then rest to allow them to heal and grow stronger. Among compulsive personalities (like mine) we feel if running 3 miles on Monday is good then running another 3 on Tuesday must be even better. This, of course, is not true. Weightlifters have known for years that they must allow at least a day of rest after working a certain muscle group if the muscles are to grow larger.

The concept of rest days holds true with aerobic exercises as well. The muscles you stress need a day to heal. Actually, I've found that as you grow older you sometimes need more than one day to recover. After really tough workouts I'll often just feel tired the day after, with no specific soreness, and then the muscles involved ache all over on the second day. I call this a second day soreness and it means I've probably whacked the particular muscles a little too much. When this happens it's wise to take an extra day off. A recent study, however, from Yokohama City University in Japan (Applied Physiology, Nutrition and Metabolism, June 2006) did show that older men could recover from hard workouts as fast as younger men. For whatever reason I just don't think I do.

Measuring the Intensity

To ensure that your aerobic workouts focus on intensity you should measure that intensity. One measure of aerobic fitness is a person's maximum oxygen uptake or volume, abbreviated as $VO_{2\,max}$. $VO_{2\,max}$ is the volume of oxygen that can be consumed when exercising at a maximum level. The fitter you are, the higher $VO_{2\,max}$ you will have, and with a higher $VO_{2\,max}$ a person can work out at a more intense level. $VO_{2\,max}$ is an excellent measure of how much blood the heart can pump.

Measuring $VO_{2\,max}$, however, is difficult without sophisticated equipment. There is fortunately a pretty close relationship between heart rate and oxygen consumption or $VO_{2\,max}$. Heart rate is very easy to measure. For most activities, heart rate will give you results similar to those gained by measuring VO_2. So, go buy a heart rate monitor. There are fancy ones for a couple of hundred dollars that beep when you go over or under set limits and can be down-loaded to a computer. I have seldom found the need for something this sophisticated and always buy a simple one. These cost around $50. They show heart rate and that is all I really want to know. You can also determine heart rate by taking your pulse as you check the minute hand of your watch. This is difficult to do while you are still exercising, but once you stop exercising, it will give you a pretty good idea of what your heart is doing. After you have worked out for years you'll probably know your approximate heart rate just by the thumping in your chest.

Maximum Heart Rates

One measure of workout effort is the percentage of your maximum heart rate at which you are performing. While maximum heart rates vary tremendously with a person's genetics and training, the estimate most often used is 220 minus your age. I'm 70 so my theoretical maximum heart rate should be 220 minus 70 or 150 beats per minute. Actually, either through genetics or years of training, my current maximum heart rate is about 138. The most accurate way to determine your maximum heart rate is to do a stress test at a medical facility that consists of running on a treadmill while hooked up to an electrocardiogram. That test can measure your pulse at the maximum

Theoretical Maximum Heart Rates at Different Ages	
Age	Theoretical Maximum Heart Rate
20	200
25	195
30	190
35	185
40	180
45	175
50	170
55	165
60	150
65	145
70	140
75	135
80	130
85	125
90	120
95	115
100	110

effort at which you can perform. If you work out frequently with a heart monitor you can find your maximum heart rate on those occasions when you are motivated to push yourself to the limit and end up gasping or vomiting or practically passing out. That point is likely to be your maximum. It is not a pleasant level to reach. Exercising at or near your maximum heart rate is a painful activity and not something you want to do very often. I find that reaching 90% of my maximum, once or twice a week, for periods ranging from a few seconds to 5 minutes, is quite sufficient.

Training Zones

Once you have calculated or estimated your maximum heart rate it's easy to tailor your workouts to be efficient. Training zones are the percentage of your maximum heart rate at which you exercise. Perhaps once a week you might want to work out at 90% of your maximum. Suppose your maximum heart rate is 160 beats, determined by the previous chart. Therefore, 90% of your 160 maximum will be 144 beats per minute. This is an intense level and will have you gasping if you stay there very long. Working out at 90% of your maximum is usually done as intervals of 30 seconds to 5 minutes each, with rest periods in between. The rest periods should be active but at a level easy enough to allow you to catch your breath. High intensity interval training or wind sprints of this sort burns lots of calories, really stresses the body and probably requires a rest day afterwards.

Working out at a more reasonable level of 80% of your maximum will improve your $VO_{2\,max}$ and improve your cardiovascular system and should be the level you attain two or three days a week. When training at this level you'll be increasing your endurance, strengthening your muscles and will still be able to function the next day. If you work out at lower rates, say in the 65% to 75% range, increase the time spent at your activity and do it several times a week. On days when you just don't "have it" or want a rest, train at 50% to 70% of max to recover. These days can be fun. Enjoy them.

Knowing your heart rate and setting a program to take advantage of training zones is key to improving your aerobic conditioning. Running or biking or any kind of aerobic activity requires work. The body is very efficient in finding ways to cheat and minimize this work. You'll hear more about cheating in the strength-training chapter but cheating is most insidious with aerobics. Without a measuring device such as a heart monitor your body will find ways to make your workouts easier and therefore less meaningful. The body is incredibly clever at this. When your body finds an easier way of doing something it negates some of the benefits you are trying to obtain. When I cycle by myself I find my body has an unalterable urge to mosey along at 14 or 15 mph with a heart rate of 70 or 75. This is only slightly more than 50% of my maximum and too low to be doing me much good. Then, if someone passes me the competitive juices spring to life and I resume a pace worthy of a workout. If the person passing me is an attractive young woman I tend to spring to life with even more enthusiasm. Sometimes this leads to a great workout with my heart rate going to the 95% level and sometimes I just get embarrassed as she disappears over the next hill.

Types of Intense Workouts

My son introduced me to an intense workout known as "stadiums" which he used when training with the Harvard Ski Team. The idea is to run up a tier of

THE STADIUM STORY

I started "running the stadiums" at Harvard 8 or 10 years ago after hearing my son talk about his training with the ski team. This is a tough workout. Most people are able to complete only 4 or 6 sections at first. After months of diligent effort I proudly completed all 37 and called my son to tell him of my accomplishment. He asked, "What was your time?" I was incredulous. Time? Who was thinking about time when you are struggling through this workout? Non-plussed he informed me that the record time was something like 17 minutes. Olympic level athletes do it in 22 minutes, top college athletes in 26 or some number like that.

Back I went and worked on my time. A year later when I gave him the numbers, which I really don't remember, he coolly asked if I had ever done a "century". By now I was probably 65 years old and had never seen a person within 15 years of my age doing this ridiculous workout. Incredulous once again, though I couldn't imagine any sane person running 100 of these things, I considered the feat. At times like this you wish for a nice non-competitive daughter. The next year I completed 50 and stopped talking to my son about these workouts.

30 seats at the Harvard Stadium, down the stairs and run up the next tier of seats. There are 37 tiers around the stadium. This is one hell of an intense workout and the very definition of intensity and rest. I do the stadiums on Tuesdays and often need 2 days of rest

before I can use my legs again. I wear a heart monitor and have a goal of reaching a heart rate of 130 at the top of each of the 37 sections. When I accomplish this I'm working at about 95% of my maximum heart rate and am wiped out for the day. I don't see many 70 year olds doing this workout.

Everyone doesn't have a stadium a few miles from their home so let's get back to the idea of intensity and rest in more typical workouts. If you are running, once a week include some sprints. You can "run telephone poles". Try sprinting for 3 telephone poles and then jog easily for 3 or until you recover. Then sprint for another 3 telephone poles. Start by repeating this 5 times. Or you can include a steep hill in your runs once a week and time your climb while measuring the intensity with a heart monitor. The same goes for biking or swimming or any other aerobic activity. Doing one minute sprints as hard as you can and then resting for a minute and repeating this 5 times is vastly more effective at improving your cardio-vascular health than riding or swimming easily for an hour. There are dozens of intense swim workouts. You can simply alternate slow and fast laps. One favorite of mine was to swim 50 or 100-yard repeats every time the minute hand hit a selected number of seconds. When you begin it's easy but as you tire the rest between sets becomes less and less and the intensity increases. Include interval workouts and sprints when you bike or swim or row but never without a rest day in between. It's easy to fall into the trap of doing a regular routine where you just expend the same effort each day. Try to avoid it.

Steep hills are perfect for intensity workouts

There are many ways to play little intensity games
with yourself no matter which aerobic activity you
choose. As long as you do them a few times a week

your aerobic conditioning will improve. This is why it's difficult to achieve serious aerobic benefits from activities like housework, golf, shopping, splashing around in a pool, or hanging sheet rock. While these and many other activities can be aerobic they are difficult to intensify. Without intensity, and better still measurable intensity, aerobic benefits are minimized. Remember to be constantly vigilant and keep your workouts honest. Your body is genetically programmed to do things in the easiest way and this reduces the efficiency of your workouts. Use your heart monitor and stop watch. Even better find a training partner. The partner is a competitor to inspire effort, and a watchdog to ensure proper form. A trainer is best but naturally involves expense and certain inconveniences.

Keeping a Log

Every coach I've ever had would bug me to keep a log and I'd resist as long as possible. But they were right. Keeping a log lets you see patterns that develop in your workouts. Logs can show you when you're tired and need days (or weeks) of rest. They give clues to causes of injury and ensure you don't slack off on workout intensity. You'll find hints on how your diet, rest and workouts affect your performance. Logs become most valuable over time when seemingly insignificant details evolve into patterns of information. Some changes, after all, only occur over long periods of time. Try it. Use any notebook and record the date, activity, times, intensity and how you felt. Add what you ate, how long you slept, your weight and anything else that might shed light on your body over periods of time. I occasionally find myself checking a log I kept 10 years ago to see how fast I did a particular route. Logs provide fascinating and valuable information.

Cross Training

Aerobic exercise is the most important activity you can do to improve the quality and length of your life. Your workouts increase in value if you diligently train with intensity and alternate this intensity with periods of rest. Cross training is another important concept. It is very easy to get into the habit of doing the same exercise over and over again. People find something they like, such as running or biking or swimming, and that becomes their primary workout. This is fine. After all, doing something you like is not only enjoyable but you're much more likely to continue doing something that's fun. But your body is going to last a lot longer and get many more benefits if you vary your training. Serious athletes use cross training. Cross training is where different activities are used to support one main sport. Bike racers will cross-country ski or skate in their off season and runners swim or row on rest days. It's a valuable concept for everyone concerned with fitness. Consider cross training as a cocktail of various workouts. It not only helps to keep more muscle groups active but it also greatly reduces the risk of injury. Cross training takes a little extra willpower since it's sometimes hard to do things you're not good at. Your proficiency is not important

You're sure this will improve my swim times?

compared to the benefits you'll gain. Another subtle benefit of cross training is the renewed excitement when you get back to your primary activity. Vary your workouts, even if you're working towards a marathon or masters swim race or bike century. Your body will thank you.

My personal experience with cross training came from competing in triathlons. By definition you are cross training with triathlons as they involve 3 events. I found while competing that I was a pretty good runner. Most of my races were won in this event. But biking is my real joy and I really don't care much for running. When I retired from serious competition, biking became my primary aerobic activity but I still try to run several times a week. This exercises different muscles and, since running is a load bearing activity, it protects against osteoporosis. Running is also useful because it's so convenient when traveling, requiring little more than shorts and running shoes. When the weather is cold or rainy and when time is short I can complete a good run workout in 30 minutes while on a bike I'm barely warmed up in that amount of time.

You should not do one thing to the exclusion of everything else. Too much running or too much of anything has its disadvantages. Everyone knows someone with knee problems. Run 25 or 30 miles every week, year in and year out, and unless the structure and alignment of your legs is perfect you are likely to join this group. Running is a high impact sport and knees are seriously at risk from this impact. The same can happen with swimming even though this is a non-impact activity. Swimmers often run into shoulder problems especially after doing the same stroke for thousands of yards. Ear infections are another risk. Biking is also a non-impact sport but serious injuries abound from falls and collisions not to mention the recently publicized impotency problems due to saddle pressure. Regardless of the activity that brings you the greatest joy vary your workouts. You'll be rewarded with better long-term fitness. Remember what the ancient Greeks said, NOTHING IN EXCESS. Alternate your workouts.

Endorphins and "Runners High"

Here is some great news for everyone working out at an intense level. There is a bio-chemical compound called endorphins that is produced by your pituitary gland and is injected from the gland directly into your

brain and spinal cord. These endorphin compounds
resemble opiates and make you feel real good. If endorphins were not naturally produced by your body, they
would most certainly be declared an illegal drug and
you'd need a prescription to get them. Think of endorphins as morphine that the body makes itself. Most,
but not all, scientists agree that strenuous exercise
stimulates the production of endorphins. For years
runners and other athletes noticed the good feeling
that came from an intense workout and started to look
forward to these endorphins and the sense of well
being that they generated. Endorphins got the name
"runners high" back in the 1970's when running and
jogging became popular.

I believe that endorphins, much like morphine, are addictive. Once your body learns how to get them, it wants them on a regular basis. I, for one, love my endorphins and find that if I have a day without a workout I feel logy and even a little depressed. So I'm an addict. Fortunately this is a rather good addiction as it keeps you always anxious for the next workout and, as this book hopes to convince you, workouts keep you looking and feeling young. If you have ever worked out intensely you probably already know the good feeling it generates. If not you are in for a wonderful surprise.

Other Aerobic Exercises

I've been talking about the common aerobic activities like running, swimming, biking and rowing. Certainly there are many others that are equally worthwhile such as cross-country skiing, aerobic dance, skipping rope and skating. Soccer, volleyball, basketball, water polo, and hockey also are high in intensity, usually continuous enough and require enough sustained effort to stimulate your cardio-vascular system. Tennis, handball, racquetball, basketball, squash, roller-blading, martial arts, ice-skating and many others also are excellent. Less beneficial are sports like baseball, scuba diving, downhill skiing, golf and easy walking where continuous and serious aerobic activity is not involved. Don't get me wrong, any activity is better than none, but sports that don't get you huffing and puffing are doing you less good. If in doubt just take a

look at the shape of people who practice the sport. You won't see many fat, out of shape runners or bikers or basketball players. There are, however, lots of toneless overweight scuba divers, golfers, and walkers.

2 Resistance Training for Strength and Muscle

As a kid growing up in Brooklyn, Charles Atlas advertised his promise of strength and power from the back of every comic book. Finally working up the courage to reply to these ads, I was bombarded with mailings to buy his *Dynamic Tension* program for a mere $35. Unfortunately, as tempting as it was, for a 9 or 10 year old, it might as well have cost $35,000. The price was way beyond the range of my 50-cent weekly allowance. As the weeks and months went by, however, special offers and discounts materialized. The course, after all, was only a series of mimeographed sheets. "Thirty dollars if you responded this week," "$25 for a summer special," "$20 holiday special." Finally, after many months, an "absolutely last" offer arrived. Five dollars. The $5 price was feasible. My best friend Howard and I each coughed up

$2.50 and we were on the way to muscular dominance of the neighborhood.

I did not become the terror of East 23rd Street. *Dynamic Tension* was a series of isometric exercises. The system involved pitting one muscle against another to create resistance. The bicep curl exercise, for example, involved pushing downward with one arm into the upturned palm of the other. While this can produce the same result as a dumbbell, it's pretty hard to regulate and quantify how hard you are working. If you remember anything from the aerobic chapter you know there will be minimum benefits without stressing the muscles and it's difficult to push yourself if you cannot measure the effort. Isometric exercise, for all its weaknesses, was my first introduction to strength training.

Why Strength Training?

Ever see someone with flabby calves or forearms? Probably not. Calves and forearms are used so often in everyday walking or grasping that they tend to stay toned. These muscles don't atrophy because they're used too much. It's different with other muscles in your body. Turn 50 or 60 without using some of them and they just give up being needed and start turning to mush. It's the same as an old lawn mower I recently came across in a corner of my garage. The thing hadn't been used in 25 years and you'd hardly expect the wheels to turn much less the engine cough to life. Muscles also "rust" or shrink when not used. Look at what happens to a limb after just a few months in a cast. Imagine the deterioration in a muscle that is barely used for 30 years. If you want to keep your body young as you age you jolly well better include some sort of resistance training in your program.

With resistance training you can minimize the loss of muscle volume and strength that usually accompanies aging. Most athletes find a decline in their performance as they age. This decline can be minimal until age 60 if you continue strength training. After 60 the decline accelerates but can still be significantly reduced by training. This chart, based on a study by Dr. Stephen Seiler*, illustrates the reduction of strength for trained and untrained men. Though based on a single exercise, my own experience indicates that this pretty much holds true for the whole body.

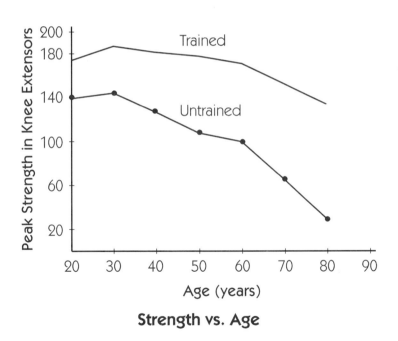

Strength vs. Age

---

*Professor, Faculty of Health and Sport, University of Agder, Norway.

The decrease in strength is probably due to the atrophy of muscle fibers caused by the body's reduced production of testosterone and growth hormones. These both decrease rapidly after age 60. While the body experiences serious reduction in muscle volume and bone density with age, you can limit these declines with some sort of strength training. The most efficient form of strength training is weight lifting.

The loss of muscle volume is particularly noticeable in the upper body.

You even see many very aerobically fit people, competitive, elite long distance runners and cyclists whose upper bodies seem emaciated. These athletes need to keep upper body weight to a minimum. For most of us this is not such a good thing. Having some muscle around your bones prevents injuries and minimizes back, neck and shoulder pain. It also gives you the strength to perform in everyday life. When my wife asks me to open an old jar from the back of a cupboard I can still wrap my hands around it and feel manly and powerful as I twist off the tight cap, at least most of the time. To a certain extent, upper body strength contributes to aerobic performance as in climbing a steep hill on a bike when your back muscles come into play. Also important, with a reasonable upper body you'll look great at the beach and trim in clothes. Looking strong and healthy is a great psychological factor in feeling young as you'll see in the "Magic of Thinking Young" chapter.

A loss of strength can also lead to an accelerated cycle of aging. When you can no longer perform some physical act that you've done all your life you feel older. Feeling older encourages you to do those actions less and that leads to further weakening. The cure is simple. Lift some weights or do some other form of strength training. The resistance training described here will keep your body looking healthy and young. Strength training will also give you the cushioning of muscle to prevent injuries. As an added bonus, increasing muscle mass increases your metabolic rate making it easier to burn calories.

Metabolic Rate

Your basal metabolic rate is the amount of energy your body burns while totally at rest. It's the amount of calories you need to keep your basic body organs like your heart, liver, lungs, brain etc. operating. This basal metabolic rate usually consumes your body's greatest quantity of calories. As you age your basal metabolic rate decreases. That means you need less calories to keep your basic functions working and if you continue to eat the same amount of calories as before, you'll gain weight. Increased cardiovascular exercise and increased muscle mass however will increase your basal metabolic rate. Muscle mass burns more calories than fat mass and weight control is much easier when you exercise.

Resistance Training

There are many kinds of resistance training. You can use weights, exercise machines, springs, bending

FINDING YOUR BODY TYPE

Scientists have divided all mankind into 3 body types. No matter how much you lift weights, diet or exercise, you can change your body type only so much.

ECTOMORPHS

This is a skinny, nervous, nerdy body type that can eat all it wants without gaining weight. Ectomorphs often wear glasses and go into professions like computers and accounting. Female ectomorphs rarely wear more than an A cup bra and male ectomorphs get sand kicked in their faces at the beach.

MESOMORPHS

These muscular people hang around gyms a lot and answer to names like Vinny, Gus or Gloria. Mesomorphs like to work with concrete and pose as Playboy centerfolds. Mesomorphs make most of the things Ectomorphs and Endomorphs use.

ENDOMORPHS

Fat, happy people responsible for most of man's profound philosophical thinking, endomorphs are very happy sitting and using their brains. Responsible for inventing things like potato chips, chocolate mousse, Lazy-Boy recliners and birthday parties, endomorphs recognize the value of having a nice, soft, round tush to sit on, and they are wise enough to take advantage of it.

bows, and even your own body weight. They all are effective and as with aerobic activities the object is to stress your muscles progressively. Weights are probably the most efficient and convenient way to do this. They allow a wide variety of motion and make increases in intensity easy to measure. Weights are inexpensive and easy to store. Using your own body weight, such as with pushups, may be even cheaper and pretty convenient when you travel but there are limits to the range of exercises you can do only using your body weight.

You'll find impressive chrome and steel machines at most gyms. Nautilus, Marcy, Yukon are a few brands and these machines can work muscle groups very effectively. They are fun and I enjoy using them. While these machines often mimic the motions of free weights they cannot stress small muscles used for connection and balance as well. Barbells will give you better results than most machines and dumbbells are better still. Dumbbells require you to balance and control the weight with each hand. This is harder than doing the same motion with both hands on a barbell and therefore more beneficial. Dumbbells simply generate more stresses. In recent years workouts have been developed incorporating lifting motions while standing on an unstable surface. These exercises generate even more stresses on small muscles and connective tissue.

I work out with weights twice a week. One day I work chest and arms, the other back and biceps. I rarely work my legs with weights since I'm doing so much biking, running and skiing I have trouble finding a rest day for my lower body. I feel my interval training in these activities stresses the legs sufficiently.

Three days of weight lifting used to be the norm amongst body builders allowing rest days between heavy workouts. Nowadays serious body builders can work out 5 or more days a week by carefully alternating the muscle groups stressed. Unless strength training or big muscles are your main goal you'll find it quite easy to keep fit and young looking with two strength workouts each week.

New Routines

As with all exercise it's best to keep varying your strength workouts and their intensity. You should keep surprising the muscles by constantly changing your routines. It's hard to do. There is something very tempting in doing the same familiar exercises and watching the increase in the weights you are able to handle. It's not the best way to train and I know I'm guilty of doing favorite exercises to the exclusion of new ones that might bring more benefits. You should try to fight this tendency.

Know Thyself

Before starting a resistance training program let some knowledgeable person take a look at your body. A trainer is great at this point but at the very least try an honest peek in the mirror. This will give you an idea of where to start and which muscles are most in need of development.

"Know Thyself" (and your limitations)

Without an honest evaluation it's easy to get side-tracked. Sometimes when I'm at a gym I notice obese and very out of shape women doing some specialized triceps exercises. There is nothing wrong with triceps exercises but there are dozens of areas these people should be attending to first. I imagine these women looked in a mirror and noticed a flabby mass hanging under their arms. Upon joining a gym they asked a trainer how to eliminate it. The trainer, anxious to please, shows them triceps exercises. What they really need is diet, aerobic exercise and a general muscle-building program. Before beginning a resistance-training program find some way to be realistic with yourself or find an outside person to suggest the areas to concentrate on.

Finding a Trainer

I've seen some older trainers who, though obviously out of shape, could devise brilliant workouts. I've also seen some young trainers who are 50 pounds over-weight and I wonder what kind of guidance you could expect from someone that looked like that. It's not easy finding a qualified trainer.

There are various trainer credentials around but I found 12 different certifying organizations on Google's first page. It's hard to figure which "diplomas" are meaningful. Many of these certification programs are nothing more than a short mail order course. I'd suggest you get personal recommendations or watch the trainer work with another client. Find a trainer who will inspire you with the way they have developed their own body or by their store of experience and knowledge.

Strength Training

There are thousands of resistance exercises using all sorts of devices. I couldn't begin to list them all. Two great books on weight lifting are *Teach Yourself*

Visually, Weight Training by Moran and *Strength Training Anatomy* by Delavier. There are also endless instructional materials on the Internet that will give you detailed information on exercise routines. On the next pages I show my basic routines. Take these just as a general introduction. Remember, it's best to keep varying your workouts so use my workouts only as a starting point.

Most trainers suggest 8 to 12 repetitions of a weight lifting movement. A repetition or "rep" is usually one up and down motion. Regardless of how many reps you do you'll get the most benefit when the exercise is done to exhaustion – the point where you absolutely cannot push the weight up again. After several sessions the number of repetitions you can perform before exhaustion will increase. When they get to around 12 you'll want to increase the weight.

Each series of 8 or 12 reps are called a "set" and I do 4 sets of each exercise. Some studies show you get almost as much benefit doing just one set to exhaustion though most serious weight lifters suggest doing several. While I do multiple sets of most exercises, see what works best for you as you become familiar with weight training. Rest about one minute between sets, longer if you are working very heavy. It is generally thought that muscular strength is developed using heavier weights and lower repetitions. The endurance of your muscles is best developed with lighter weights and higher reps.

Weightlifters often divide their workouts into chest-arms days and biceps-back-leg days. This has worked fine for me.

Resistance Training for Strength and Muscle

Chest and Arm Workout

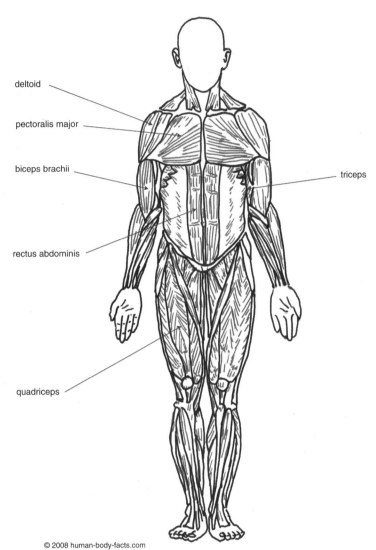

deltoid

pectoralis major

biceps brachii

triceps

rectus abdominis

quadriceps

Die Young ... as late as possible 32

Dumbbell bench press

Your arms in the starting position should really be lower than shown here. Due to a recent shoulder operation my range of motion was limited when these photos were taken. This exercise uses your pectoalis major, the main chest muscle as well as the shoulder's anterior deltoid and triceps.

START

FINISH

Incline dumbbell press   4 sets
The incline bench press works the upper portion of the
"pecs" somewhat more than the regular bench press.

START

FINISH

Seated Arnold press   4 sets
This press gets all 3 parts of your deltoids and triceps. You start with the hands turned towards your face twisting them outward as you lift. It's named for Arnold Schwarzenegger and visualizing his bulk always inspires me.

START

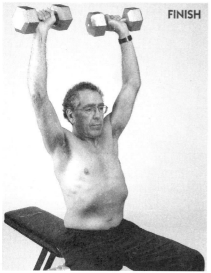

FINISH

Chest fly on ball   *4 sets*

Flys work the pectoral muscles and can also be done on a bench. The ball introduces some instability that makes the movement a bit harder.

START

FINISH

French triceps curl   4 sets

This is a pure triceps exercise and can be done with
your hands facing up or towards each other. The movement should start near your forehead and end with the
elbows as close together as possible.

START

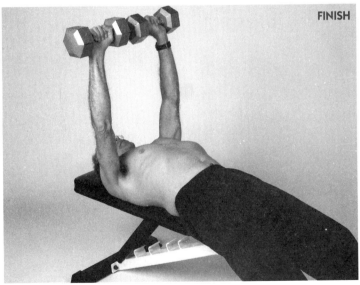

FINISH

Lateral dumbbell raise   4 sets
This works your deltoids and upper trapezius. I often alternate these with the Front arm raises, which uses the deltoids and upper pectorals.

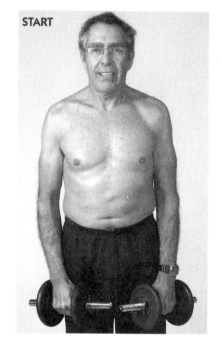

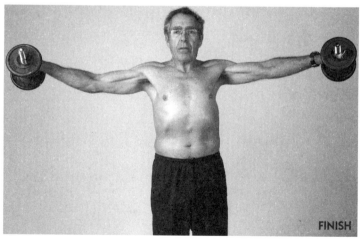

I try to vary these basic movements with alternatives. I also try to vary the workouts by switching from heavy weights with low repetitions to lighter weights with high reps.

Back and Bicep Workout

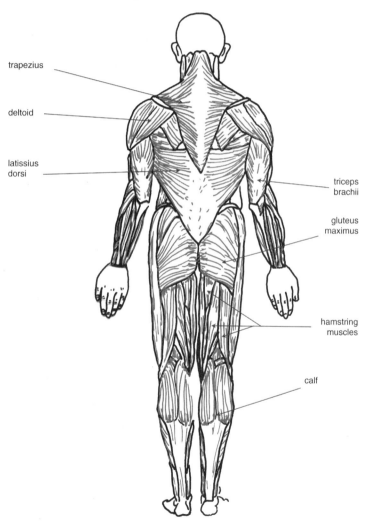

trapezius

deltoid

latissius dorsi

triceps brachii

gluteus maximus

hamstring muscles

calf

One arm dumbbell rows

The one arm row mainly works the latissimus dorsi, the large back muscle, as well as your trapezius, rhomboid and a bit of your deltoid and biceps. Alternate arms.

Lat pull downs
If you have a machine available this is an excellent
Lat exercise. You can get similar benefits from using
a chinning bar.

START

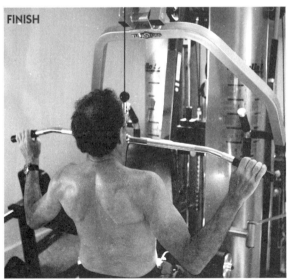

FINISH

Alternate arm dumbbell curl
Doing this classic biceps exercise in a seated position
prevents you from swinging your body to make it easier.

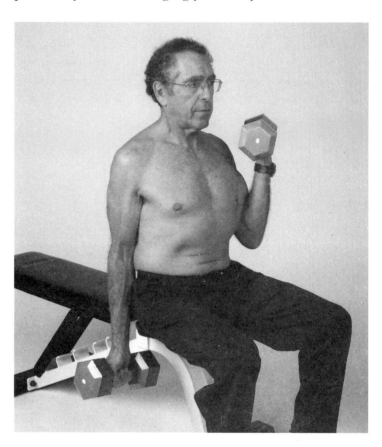

Dead lifts

Keep your head up and start the lift using your legs. This is a power lifting movement that gets many leg and back muscles.

START

FINISH

Seated rows

If a machine is available, this exercise works almost your entire back. You can substitute bent rows that are done holding a bar with the back straight while bending the waist at 45 degrees. Bring the bar to your chest.

START

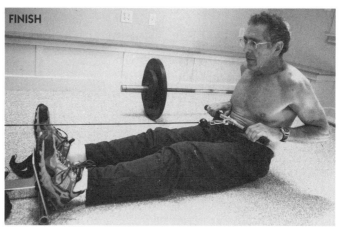

FINISH

Upright row
This works your deltoids and trapezius

Each of the chest and arm or back and bicep workouts take me about an hour. If you want to add something for your legs, squats are a great exercise. Squats also build back and hip strength as well as being a super lower body workout. If your primary activities, such as swimming, are not working your legs very much, you will definitely want to include squats and other leg exercises.

Squats

Squats are one of the best exercises for your legs and back and it's unfortunate that many people hate (myself included) to perform them. Your thighs should be horizontal to the floor at the finish.

FINISH

Cheating

Doing a weight lifting movement in the proper form is much more important than heaving up the heaviest possible weight. With most weight training it's pretty easy to cheat. Cheating usually involves using one of the body's bigger muscles to help do a movement and it defeats much of the value of the exercise. Swinging the weight with your hip and back muscles when doing a barbell curl is one example. Bending your knees and pushing a little with your legs when doing an overhead press is another. You can fight the tendency to cheat by working out with a partner or a trainer. Watching your movements in a mirror may also help, or perform the movement in a sitting position where it is hard to bring your legs and hips into the motion. Using poor form may enable you to put up larger weight but it is a losing game for stressing your muscle.

In Summary

One truth I've found with pretty much all exercises. It's usually the ones you hate the most that provide the important benefits. I, for example, dislike dead lifts and heavy dumbbell bench press routines. These are among the most beneficial for me. With aerobic programs I positively dread intervals and repeated hill climbs and these are vastly more effective than a lazy run or bike ride. It's not easy avoiding the habit of doing the easy and favorite activities. Fight this. To realize your goal of staying young keep varying your workouts and keep intensifying them.

Strength training is relatively simple. Work the muscles of your upper body a couple of times a week. If you're a little sore the next day you are stimulating your muscles sufficiently and they will grow stronger. If you feel no stiffness the day after a workout you should increase the weight or number of repetitions.

Just as intensity and rest are the keys to aerobic training they are equally important to resistance training. One advantage with resistance training is that it is easy to measure the intensity. If you push up heavier weights you are getting stronger and if you hurt the day after a workout you'll likely be reminded to take a day off. Just remember that intensity is the key to improvement. Even if you are growing too old to be bothered about looking great at a beach, intensity is also the key to muscle maintenance.

There are endless exercises and movements using resistance and weights to build your muscles and strength. Any gym or book on the subject will show you more than you can do in a lifetime. Just remember the two basic ideas of this book: nothing in excess and intensity and rest.

3 CORE

Looking out from my office window, fifteen or twenty years ago, I noticed a new tenant shuffling to his factory's entrance. The poor fellow was obese and hunched over with movements painfully slow. He seemed a very old man. Later after getting to know him I learned his constant back pain led to his shuffling gait, poor posture and inability to exercise. To my amazement I also learned that this "old man" and I were the same age. We had similar backgrounds all our lives and graduated from M.I.T. in the same year. He appeared 20 years older than me and it was doubtful he had been able to do any exercise in years. Here was a perfect example of "dying old and as soon as possible." This poor guy was suffering from a totally unstable core making him "old" while I was leading an active and full life.

What is Core?

Core is a hot topic these days. You see articles about core in every newspaper, magazine and certainly every publication that has something to do with fitness. Core is the mass in your middle. It's your center of gravity. It's the area of your trunk and pelvis and it consists of 29, mostly small, muscles. Core is where all your body movements originate. It's a source of power. Other than "6 pack abs" it's pretty hard to see and measure your core, but it braces your back, stabilizes and balances your body, holding it all together, and even affects your digestive system.

Your core is made up of 29, mostly small, muscles

Believe me, it is a key to staying young. Here is a
story about one of my experiences.

Why Work Your Core?

Shortly after I was first married, some 42 years ago, my
lower back "went out". I was hunched over in pain,
and effectively crippled as far as any normal activities were concerned. I tried bed rest and boards under
my mattress. I took pain relievers. I went to chiroprac-
tors. Their manipulations could relieve the spasms or
tightening of the lower back muscles for a few hours
or days but the "bad back" always returned. Finally
(these were the days before you needed referrals from
your primary care physician) I went for 3 days of tests
at the famous Lahey Clinic. At the end of all the
examinations and x-rays the doctor sat me down and
explained that I had some degenerate discs in my
back. He gave me some exercises to do and cautioned
that I'd eventually need an operation to fuse the discs.

The exercises were the basic back stuff; lying on
your back and bringing the knees up to your chest, sit
ups with bent knees, squeezing your buttocks together
and pressing the small of your back into the floor. I
did them religiously. I added to them, experimented,
invented new ones and gradually built the strength of
the muscles surrounding my lower back. I expanded
these exercises as my back became stronger to include
some that are positively forbidden to people with back
problems. Stuff like heavy dead lifts and back arches
with weight from a prone position. Gradually I stopped
having back pains.

About a year ago I went for one of those diagnostic body scans, the controversial kind your insurance won't cover and you have to pay for by yourself. In my case it cost $1,200 but they did give me a "free", thick terrycloth bathrobe that I've become very fond of. After the scans the radiologist sat me down to go over the results. He asked if I suffered from back pain. As I shook my head no, he pointed to the degenerate discs in my lower back and indeed, even to a layman's eyes, they looked very worn. He next looked more carefully at the area and said, "Well it seems the muscles surrounding the vertebra are holding them in place." I had developed my core without ever knowing the word.

There's your motivation for reading this chapter. Forty-eight major nerves come through the center of your spine. These nerves are the network that connects the brain with your body. A strong core will support and protect your spine and prevent pain by keeping the spinal bones from pinching these nerves. An exercised core will improve your posture and balance, eliminate injuries to other parts of your body and have you feeling years younger. A strong core provides a powerful platform for all your activities. About 30% of the population complains of back problems. It's the most common side-effect of a weak core. Your core is the foundation of the entire skeletal structure of the body. Additionally your core acts as a protective wall supporting your internal organs. When you exercise your core, these internal organs are utilized and stimulated, preventing them from adhering together. Your entire digestive system and bowels will work better.

My Core Exercises

Here are the core exercises that I do. I combine these with the stretching exercises shown in the next chapter. Some I do every day as stretches and some two or three times a week as muscle builders.

Bent knee sit up
More a stretch than a muscle builder, remember to reach as your arms move between your legs.

START

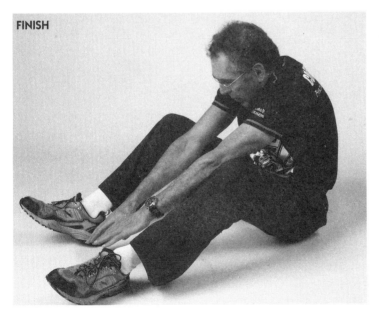
FINISH

Leg side to side
I did these for years thinking they would reduce some small "love handles" a date once mentioned. The "handles" stayed until I changed my diet a few years ago.

Crunches on ball

I do hundreds of these crunches a couple of times each week.

START

FINISH

Ball pass

Passing the ball between your hands and feet works both the lower and upper abdominals.

START

FINISH

Sit-ups on Roman Chair
I bought this Roman Chair for $99 and do twisting
sit-ups a couple of times each week.

START

FINISH

Twisting back arches on Roman Chair
I twist right, lower my torso and then twist left. Great for your lower back.

START

FINISH

Back extensions on Roman Chair
This exercise can also be done on an inflatable ball with your legs braced against a wall. I've worked up to doing it holding a weight behind my head.

Crunch with legs

Doing a conventional crunch while bringing your knees to meet your upper torso creates a powerful core exercise. You can twist as you crunch with right elbow going to the left knee and vise versa.

START

FINISH

I do only one set of some of these core movements when using them as stretches. About twice each week I'll do multiple sets as a real core workout. I'm rarely sore the next day which may be an indication that I'm not working with enough intensity. On the other hand my middle is strong, my back pain free, my stomach flat and my digestive system works just fine. I'm very satisfied with the results.

When doing crunch exercises some trainers recommend engaging your inner abdominals. These inner abdominals are the ones you feel when you cough. You engage them by coughing and holding them tight during your movements. You don't need lots of equipment to build a strong core. A $29 inflatable ball is enough and they all come with a list of exercises.

Balance and Instability Exercises

Instability exercises utilize balls, half domes, balance cushions, rollers, balance boards, rocker boards and other devices. Recently a whole new genre of exercises

*Instability surfaces introduce stress
to many small connective tissues*

have become popular utilizing these tools. Movements performed on balance boards and other instable surfaces stress and develop many small connecting muscles, tendons and ligaments. These small muscles and connectors are particularly valuable in making older persons less vulnerable to injuries from falls or sudden movements. Working on unstable surfaces is particularly good for your core. Instability exercises are also useful with weight training and I am always impressed watching advanced athletes lifting weights while balancing on some wobbling hunk of plastic. I've started to use several unstable surfaces in my workouts and they introduce a staggering new range of exercises to stimulate muscles you never thought you had.

Choosing Core Exercises

There are many, many different core exercises. The core muscles, tendons and ligaments are more difficult to see and measure than the larger muscles of your chest, arms back and legs. I don't know exactly which exercises have eliminated my back problems so I try to do a wide variety and change them often. Aerobic exercise is easy to quantify. As long as you're breathing hard you're probably doing yourself some good. Strength training is also simple to see and measure. Not so with the core. Much of the core lies hidden. To be certain you're sufficiently stressing and strengthening your core you should explore and experiment. Physical therapists, coaches and sport literature constantly come up with new exercises. If the movements feels right and time allows, add them to your routine.

If you want more core exercises just type "c
workouts" into Google and you'll find more mo
than you ever believed existed. If you prefer
the Pilates system provides excellent core

Taking care of your core may not help you
longer but it will definitely help you live younger. ı
weak core is unable to support your internal organs.
Once they start to droop you'll have problems with
your back and everything else on your insides. Using
the unsupported trunk of your body in almost any
movement will stimulate and exercise your core. Core
workouts take little equipment and can easily be
incorporated into your daily routine. They pay divi-
dends far out of proportion to their effort.

4 Stretching to Keep Your Flexibility

Actually, I'm not the most flexible person in the world. Perhaps it is genetic. My sons are not that flexible either. When I attend a yoga class I try to hide in the back row and hope there are no mirrors. Aging reduces your flexibility and I've certainly become less flexible over the years. As connective tissue becomes less elastic it limits the range of motion of your tendons and muscles. Stretching can restore some of this range of motion and flexibility, though some studies show stretching increases the stretch tolerance of muscles and not the range of motion.

Increased flexibility can improve performance in many sports. It would also seem reasonable that increased flexibility would reduce the frequency and severity of injury though many studies disagree. I do know recent research has shown that stretching just

before activities does not prevent injuries. Current thought suggests it is better to warm up the muscles with some sort of aerobics like jumping rope or jogging before an activity and then to stretch afterwards when the muscles are warm.

Stretching versus Warming Up

Many athletes stretch especially before a competition. Some recent studies, however, suggest that stretching before an activity may actually decrease performance. It's possible stretching can reduce the maximum force your muscles can generate for a period of time. Just another myth destroyed along with your high school coach's insisting that drinking water during a workout would cause cramps. Warming up, however, before a competition or even when doing your daily stretching is not controversial. You should always strive to warm up with some sort of aerobic movements. This will increase your heart rate

and blood flow to your muscles and start to loosen them and increase their flexibility.

The warm up before stretching can be done by light exercise like jogging, jumping jacks, jumping rope or even a hot shower. This will increase the flow of blood to the muscles and start to loosen them and increase their flexibility. Each morning I combine some core exercises with my stretches. I think this combination gives my body a little time to warm up so as to make the stretches more effective. My core and stretching workout takes about 20 minutes. People will show you new stretches all

the time. Unless you want to spend your entire day stretching pick and chose those you add to your routine carefully.

How To Stretch

Slowly stretching a muscle or tendon and holding the stretched position is called a passive or static stretch. Studies vary as to how long to hold the stretch but 10 to 30 seconds are commonly advised. This kind of stretching involves slowly elongating the muscles and tendons by specific easy movement. You hold that position while consciously breathing as you attempt to move or reach a little further. This kind of stretch is thought to be safe and most beneficial. You should feel some tension as you stretch but if it becomes painful you've gone too far. A good description of what you should strive for is "mild tension".

Unlike strength building exercises, next day soreness with stretching is not thought to be a good thing. If you are sore it might mean you have overstretched and you should go easier on your muscles.

Stretching and Breathing

Some techniques, especially yoga, emphasize breathing while stretching and it is important to remember not to hold your breath. This incidentally is important in all sports especially when you're straining or nervous. Holding your breath when frightened or tense can really reduce your performance. I've never been fully convinced that breathing by expanding your diaphragm with your lungs or stomach and exhaling or inhaling specifically from your nose or mouth mattered. I just breathe deeply. Yoga, Sumo wrestlers and other disciplines would vehemently disagree. Regardless of how you breathe, it's important to keep breathing evenly and not to hold it.

A Stretch for Back Pain

Here is a stretching story that has helped me with a specific problem. About 20 years ago I found a cure for back spasms. At that time I occasionally had problems with my lower back. One day it went into spasm during a tennis game. I painfully made my way to my bedroom, sort of collapsed on the floor and managed to hook my legs over the edge of the bed before falling asleep in that position. I awoke about 20 minutes later and very gingerly stood up. To my amazement the spasm had vanished. I mentioned this to my coach and she found this "cure" perfectly logical. "In that position all your weight was pressing the small of your back into the ground. That pressure would flatten your back and stretch the tightened muscles that were causing the spasm." In addition she said, "Your back was in the lowest possible position and the maximum amount of blood was flowing there." I further suspected that by falling asleep I totally relaxed and let the stretching do its work.

Ever since that day I've used this "cure" whenever I have lower back pain and have always been successful. I've also passed this method on to anyone who complained to me of back problems. I'll admit very few of the recipients of this free advice have called the next day extolling my genius so perhaps it only works for me. It's worth trying, regardless, if you have a back spasm and here is what the position looks like.

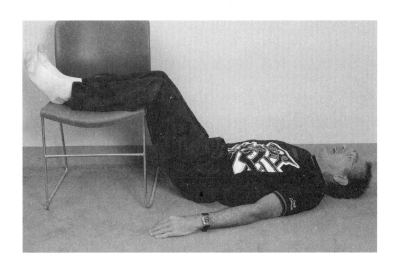

Types of Stretches

There are an endless variety of stretches. I found 7 kinds of stretching on one Internet site including ballistic, dynamic, active, passive, static, isometric and PNF. PNF incidentally stands for Proprioceptive Neuromuscular Facilitation whatever that is. Most of the descriptions were too specialized and too specific to be included in a general fitness book. Some of these "advanced" stretches include dynamic move-ments that few professional coaches recommend. A dynamic movement involves repeated bouncing actions and I suggest you start with the generally accepted simple passive stretching. You can easily expand into more sophisticated varieties if you think them beneficial.

There are about 639 skeletal muscles in the body and likely several stretches for each of them. Here are a few that I do, often combined with my core workouts. You might start with these and expand to ones that fit your activity interests and needs.

Knees to chest
I do this religiously every morning holding the position for a count of 6 and repeating it 12 times.

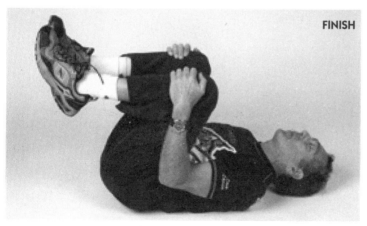

Pushing lower back into floor
Squeeze your buttocks together as you press the small of your back into the floor.

Bent knee side stretch
Lift your left leg over the right one and use it to pull the right leg towards the floor. Alternate legs.

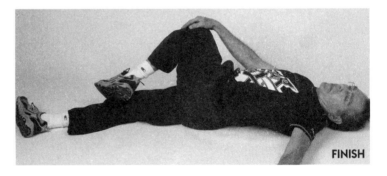

Back stretch (between door)
I hold this stretch for the count of 50 and it loosens
my back for the leg overhead, which I do next.

Leg overhead stretch
Most people can touch the ground with their toes but
I don't even come close. Hanging out in this position
and wiggling your legs stretches your lower back.

Wall stretch
This stretch feels great and takes no effort at all as it uses the weight of your body to flatten the small of your back into the floor. I separate my legs after 20 seconds to stretch the groin and then bend my knees to stretch it even more.

START

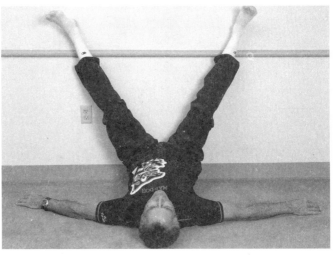

FINISH

Lower back stretch
Cross one leg over the knee of the other and pull that knee towards your chest. Alternate with the other leg.

Quad stretch
This stretches the quad and knee. An alternative is to do it lying on your stomach.

Achilles and calf stretch
Alternate the back foot that is the one being stretched.
Placing the ball of your foot on a stair and lowering
your heel can also stretch your Achilles and calf.

Butt and hip stretch
This stretches your groin, hamstrings and hip.

Neck stretches

I twist and stretch my neck from side to side and front to back creating some resistance with my hands. This strengthens the neck, preventing injuries from falls.

START

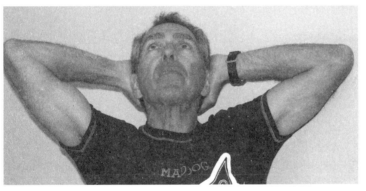

FINISH

Shoulder stretch
My wife always thinks I'm praying when she catches me doing this stretch.

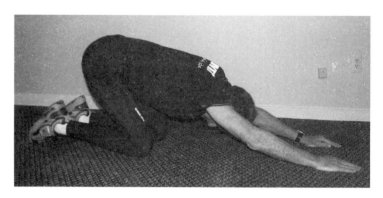

Stretching to Keep From Shrinking

A few years ago I was being fitted for an extravagant custom-made Seven Cycles bicycle and the fellow taking my measurements announced I was 5' 9" tall. I immediately protested, offering to show driver's license and army papers proving I was 5' 10" tall. After a stand-off lasting several minutes he called Rob Vandermark the owner and chief designer to check the measurement. He unfortunately agreed I was 5' 9" though he did offer to add ¼". Dejected, I realized the cartilage, called a disc, between my vertebrae was compressing with age and I resigned myself to living an inch shorter. Unfortunately at this year's annual physical the nurse announced I was 5' 8". Well I was not about to take this lying down and returned to the doctor's office with a tape measure to check his height device. It was right on. This is not a pleasant phenomena but I guess you just shrink with age. I wish I could promise that stretching will correct this very unfair aspect of growing older but try as I may I have not been successful. Coincidently, my feet seem to be growing larger each year which is tolerable if expensive with regards to ski boots.

Yoga

Yoga classes are an excellent way to be introduced to a program of stretching. As with all kinds of stretching, yoga should not be painful. Find a yoga instructor who has been certified through the Yoga Alliance and one who spends time helping the students rather than just working out themselves. Don't expect yoga to improve your aerobic conditioning, help you lose weight or increase your strength. It will aid your flexibility and perhaps improve your psychological state but is not, as some styles claim, a complete exercise program.

As I have mentioned I am not particularly flexible. I do know that doing several different stretches

for the same muscle seems to be more effective than a single one. You will do well to seek additional sources showing large numbers of different movements. One of the best books on the subject is *Stretching* by Bob Anderson. It's a great source for information on specific stretches.

5 The Magic of Thinking Young

I met with a new physician some years ago. He asked what sports I did and nodded favorably as I listed the biking, running, swimming and weight lifting. At the end of the conversation I mentioned I'd recently taken up Karate. He dismissed that with "Oh, that's only for your head." I was disappointed because

I enjoyed the confident feeling from learning to fight. While he might not have been impressed with the aerobic or strength building benefits of karate, he was dead wrong in denying the importance of "your head." In finding ways to stay young your head might just be the most important part.

The old Tenth Mountain Division fellow from the Introduction listed three things that keep you young: "You gotta be athletic, optimistic and heroic." I pondered what he meant by "heroic" for a long time. Finally I surmised that heroic referred to a youthful mental attitude. To be young you have to think young. It's much easier to think young if you do young things and hang out with young people. To be young perhaps you have to do silly things, immature things, even things that are considered foolhardy or somewhat dangerous for "older people." I think doing this kind of youthful crazy activity is what he meant by "heroic."

Corbet's Couloir

Some years ago I jumped into Corbet's Couloir at Jackson Hole Ski Area. For those of you who never skied Jackson, Corbet's is a steep run off the top of the mountain that is entered by a vertical drop of 15 or 20 feet. Well, to be honest it may really be only 10 or 15 feet, depending on snow conditions, but when you are standing on top of this steep narrow run it seems a lot higher. With just a few days left on our vacation I jumped in and hurt my knee a bit when landing. Rejoining my wife that evening, limping a little, she asked what had happened. After telling her about

Corbet's, to my surprise, she got angry. "What a stupid thing to do. Why on earth would you do something like that at your age?" "Cause it's cool and because our kids will think it's cool." I answered. "No they won't." she said and immediately phoned our sons. "Dad jumped into Corbet's today. Don't you think that was stupid?" Well, my 30-ish sons both thought that was an exceedingly impressive thing to do. My knee felt better in a few days and I've felt 10 years younger ever since especially when I "modestly" mention the feat to other skiers at appropriate occasions.

Deciding You're "Too Old"

Once you start saying, "Oh, I'm too old to do that" you will be. Too old to downhill ski or complete a marathon or play tennis with 20 year olds? You will be. Once you think age is limiting some of your activities you can be damn sure that's exactly what you can expect. You'll be too old. I participate in a martial arts form known as Brazilian Jiu Jitsu. It's mostly ground fighting similar to wrestling. Most of the students are in their 20's and 30's and after rolling around on the mat with these guys I often hurt for 2 days. Is it worth it? You bet. It would be worthwhile just to see the expressions on their faces when I tell them I'm 70. The powerful feeling I get when tapping out some 20 year old who might outweigh me by 40 lbs. is an added bonus. Admittedly I do realize that they are probably feeling guilty and taking it easy on the "old guy" who is usually their grandfather's age.

Anytime you hear someone refrain from an activity because they're too old they are creating a self-fulfilling prophecy. Think you're too old to box or play football or bicycle across the country and by gosh you are. Once a year I'll bike from my ski place in Vermont to my home outside Boston. It's a 150-mile hilly ride and sometimes, in hot weather, a quite unpleasant way to spend the day. After completing the ride I'll feel tired for a week. So why do it? Well, it's become sort of an annual tradition to convince myself I'm not growing older. I've been doing it for over 10 years and indeed, this year took half an hour off my best time. Felt younger? I certainly did.

Attitudes That Age You

My wife and I have many friends our age and younger. They are incredulous at the active lifestyle we enjoy. To most of them exercise is a slow walk or round of golf. But more than that they have grown old by their attitudes. Some are fearful of tall buildings (terrorist attacks), some driving on a high mountain road (air too thin to breathe), some swimming in the ocean (sharks, of course), some touring Third World countries (kidnappers, you know). None of these friends would ski in the trees, take a long bike ride, enter an athletic competition or even work out at a gym. How can you stay young when you think like a helpless old person?

Mental Imaging

The Inner Game of Tennis by Timothy Gallwey, published years ago, was, perhaps the first popular book on sport mental imaging. The book generated similar ones on golf and other sports and was instrumental in leading to an entirely new way of looking at how the mind could affect the body's physical state. All of these books and indeed an entire industry grew around the power of the mind for improving everything from sport performance to injury healing. Studies have shown that visualizing a good tennis shot or sinking a basketball from a foul line is just as effective as actually practicing the act. Your mind can be channeled to do the same thing with aging. It won't replace exercise and good nutrition, but combined with those it will go a long way to fulfilling your goal of staying young as late as possible.

You've undoubtedly heard of the placebo effect in the medical field. It is estimated that 30% of patients can be cured by *anything*. Believe a pill or procedure or food will cure something and it very often does. It's just another example of the power of your mind. Decide

Visualization helps you meet your goals

you're going to stay young until you die. With the added power of a healthy lifestyle, by God you will.

A good friend recently underwent double knee replacement surgery. This is a brutal operation. The very up-to-date medical team working on him taught him, in a mental imaging program, to visualize the healing process and the fulfillment of his goal to ski again that winter. He reached that goal. This is standard practice in sophisticated medical circles because it's been found to aid in the healing. Learn to use your brain the same way and you can take years off your chronological age.

Acting and Thinking Young

What constitutes "thinking young" varies with each person. Some years ago my friend Willie Weir, a bicycle traveler and writer, did an article on what constituted an adventure. Willie travels the world by bicycle and indeed in some remote areas like Albania has had some genuine life threatening adventures. He pointed out that the organized bicycle tours he once led could hardly be classified as an adventure. Everything, after all, was organized, safe and totally predictable. But, he recounted one story on a tour he led. After the introductions and bike fittings, one woman approached him quietly and confessed she hadn't been on a bike since childhood and knew nothing about how a modern bike worked or handled. Was that trip an adventure for that woman? It certainly was and she was "thinking young" and being heroic signing up for it.

Think young, act young and don't let anyone tell you that you are too old to do something. A few years ago I was sitting in my hot tub after a good day of skiing. I have a rope hanging from the ceiling to aid entering and leaving the sunken tub. A 10-year old neighbor's son had joined me and was swinging on that rope. The boy was yelling "Tarzan, Tarzan king of the jungle" as he swung and dropped into the water. He didn't notice my flinching as he missed the sharp edges and walls by inches. Finally he asked, "Herb, are you too old to swing on the rope?" I was shocked that this youngster would consider me old and a few seconds later was swinging with him and enjoying it every bit as much as he did.

When my sons were young I vowed never to refuse to ski a tough pitch with them. I've kept that vow though at times faced some terrifying runs. They have both become competent mountain bikers and have the broken collarbones, ribs and punctured lungs to prove it. I've wisely elected not to expand my vow to that sport. I do enjoy downhill-mountain biking but I'm also mature enough to avoid the expert runs. Do the crazy foolish things that youngsters do. Just keep the dangers in perspective. Don't be intimidated by Bungee jumps, heli-skiing, shark dives, polar bear swims, sky diving or age group competitions. But keep it in perspective. You're trying to add years to your life, not kill yourself.

The ideas in this chapter don't require equipment or sweat. They require only a "heroic" mental attitude and that will do as much as anything to let you die young—as late as possible.

If you're not living on the edge—you're taking up too much room.

6 Nutrition

Exercise is still the key component for staying young and your mental attitude, discussed in the last chapter, is also an important part of keeping your youthfulness. Along with those, proper nutrition will go a long way in helping you to achieve your goal. Nutrition "ain't" easy. They keep changing it. A few years ago margarine was good and butter bad. Now sticks of margarine are poison and butter not so bad. Eggs have migrated from cholesterol death to one of the most nutritious foods you can find. In 1981 coffee was thought to cause pancreatic cancer but 5 years later it was felt to prevent it. The complexity of the human body makes it hard to understand just how eating what will effect you. On top of this in the academic world success is measured by how much you publish. By testing a small number of people with almost anything, academia can produce a report about eating one thing or another that will cure or cause something. The academics get their paper and we get confused. On top of this lots of companies make money selling us things to eat and pills to pop. They make loads of promises about taste, benefits and health that are often based on extremely flimsy evidence.

I subscribe basically to the "Bubba" theory of nutrition. Eat stuff that your grandmother would recognize and recommend. This presumes you have a real old world grandmother and not a new fangled modern one who smokes and drinks and eats potato chips. Hopefully, also, your grandmother didn't fry chicken fat pieces in bacon fat to make a breakfast treat. The kind of grandmother I'm thinking of would eschew fried foods, mysterious packaged stuff and sugary candy-like things. She would approve of whole grained fresh foods, vegetables and possibly traditional old world basics like bulgur, tofu, yogurt or

kasha. Fortunately these foods are now coming back into favor and are available at local supermarkets. She'd probably be suspicious of farmed fish, vitamin laced water, low carb diets and funny colored chips. I doubt she'd suggest soda or various carbonated drinks. Depending on her ethnic background she'd prefer tea, milk, juices or perhaps red wine. You should listen to her. Her advice is sounder than ads pushing "crispy", "real food" or low fat this or that.

A few years ago I hired a personal trainer. One of the first things he did was have me keep a record of my diet. I was in great shape. My body fat was around 12%, weight 160 for my then 5'10" height and between my biking, swimming, martial arts, running and weight lifting I was probably working out 9 times a week. I was eating an enormous breakfast, skimping on lunch, having a large dinner and then indulging in dessert just before going to sleep. This trainer, to whom I'll be eternally grateful, informed me I was actually storing fat because I was eating too little and at the wrong times. He had me add two snacks each day, forbid skipping lunch and eliminated that dessert just before bedtime. As thin and healthy as I was, my diet was incorrect. The trainer felt, with my very active life style, I was not getting enough calories. He thought my body was in a somewhat starvation mode and hoarding fat to counteract this. The late night snack came a few hours after a big dinner and at an inactive time. My body would just say "Hey here comes some fuel and we're always short of fuel and we don't need it right now. Let's store it as fat." I made the changes he suggested. Though actually eating more, my weight stayed the same and within a few weeks my already low body fat dropped 25%. And these are accurate body fat figures based on a sophisticated scanning machine. My overall energy and strength stayed the same.

Why did I tell this story? I suppose to show how quickly diet changes can affect our bodies. I've always tried to eat a healthy diet but in recent years, at least to my wife, have become a fanatical bore about it. Perhaps it is because it's such an easy way to contribute to staying young.

Nutrition is a big part of maintaining your youth. While doing the research for this chapter I read *The China Study*, a very excellent and provocative book by Dr. T. Colin Campbell that claims to be the most comprehensive study of nutrition ever conducted. In this book he shows the association between heart disease, cancer and other serious maladies associated with the affluent diet of the Western World. I came to agree with him that many of the diseases in our first world countries are the result of our excessively rich animal fat and animal protein diets. Many of these killers are practically unknown in poor countries where the people live on diets primarily made up of whole grains and vegetables with animal products used in small quantities mainly as flavoring. Perhaps Campbell is right and these animal and dairy products are responsible for most of our health problems. Other studies associate the so-called "Western Diseases" with high consumption of sugar and highly refined grains. Likely both views are somewhat correct. It's wise to switch to whole grains, reduce sugar intake and use animal protein sparingly.

I've been starting to incorporate some of these ideas into my diet. I've cut down on the eggs at breakfast. Lunches and snacks center more on stuff like hummus, tofu, peanut butter, vegetables and wholewheat crackers. I'm avoiding red meats and cutting my portions of chicken and fish in half making up the caloric difference with more grains and veggies. I've reduced my intake of milk products. The initial results have been a few pounds weight loss with no decrease in strength or aerobic capacities. My cholesterol has dropped significantly and my body fat dropped 10% percent within a few weeks.

What I Eat

I've given up almost anything that's not whole grain. I've grown to love brown rice, whole wheat bread, and whole-wheat pasta (okay, so not whole-wheat pasta which tastes a bit like straw). Bulgur, whole-wheat couscous, kasha, and spelt all make interesting grain variations. I try to limit eating meat; too much saturated fat and too many links to cancer and heart disease. While I mostly eat fish and poultry I'm not so fanatical as to refuse those delicious little lamb chops they sometimes serve as hors d'oeuvres at weddings. Having a family

history with lots of cancer I gobble down any fruit or vegetable touted as a preventative tending to believe almost any study in this area.

I try to eat blackberries, blueberries, carrots, broccoli, spinach and processed tomatoes every day hoping their antioxidant claims are true. Other studies suggest benefits from tea, garlic and onions and I make those a frequent part of my diet. Breakfasts are a mixture of in-season fruit along with hot cereals in winter and cold in summer. When I have eggs I usually dilute real eggs with egg whites. For lunches I often have salmon, sardines or tuna on whole wheat breads or fruit with yogurt and cottage cheese. Dinners are often combinations of brown rice or other whole grains with tofu, vegetables and small portions of chicken, fish or tempeh.

It's tough to eat totally healthy food when going out. Butter and other fats just make food taste too good and restaurants want their food to taste good. Rather than become frantic when dining out I relax and enjoy ordering the healthiest things possible. I'll usually try to balance it out the next day at home. There are exceptions. Some restaurants take pride in cooking nutritious foods and I've had some great and imaginative meals in health-food and Asian restaurants.

Most of the beef, chicken and farmed fish offered at the supermarket in the Western World are raised on corn products. Animals fed this diet, rather than a natural one based on grass, insects or krill have flesh with altered characteristics. Studies suggest that perhaps the altering of the Omega 3 to Omega 6 balance in these foods is the cause of various cancers and heart disease. See page 106 for more on the Omega's.

The Components of Your Diet

Carbohydrates

Carbohydrates are the main fuel used when you exercise. The best sources are fruits, vegetables and whole grains. These foods also provide fiber, vitamins and minerals. Carbohydrates are stored in the muscles as a form of sugar called glycogen. The body has about 2 hours' worth of glycogen stored in its muscles, and once that is depleted you experience fatigue. The body can continue to perform by burning fat and there is enough energy stored as fat to keep you going a long time. You can train the body, somewhat, to become more adapt at burning fat by pushing your body to work through the fatigue caused by your glycogen depletion.

"How come you never run after you carbo load?"

In the old days carbohydrates were classified as simple or complex. Simple carbohydrates were sugars: fructose, dextrose, glucose and sucrose. These were considered bad carbohydrates because they broke down into digestible form quickly. Complex carbohydrates like pasta, bread and vegetables were considered "good" because they had to be first converted into sugars for the body to absorb. This made them enter the blood stream at a slower rate.

Nowadays, carbohydrates are classified by the Glycemic Index. This measures how much your blood sugar increases after eating a carbohydrate. A high glycemic food causes a fast increase in blood sugar levels. This fast increase has been linked to heart disease and diabetes. Refined and processed foods have a higher Glycemic Index.

Foods with lower Glycemic Index
    Most beans and legumes
    Fruits and vegetables containing high amounts of
        fiber
    Bran cereals
    Brown rice
    Oatmeal
    Whole grain breads and pasta
    Bulgur and barley

Foods with higher Glycemic Index
    Potatoes
    Refined cereals
    Candy
    White rice
    White pasta

You can get an idea of how the Glycemic index works from this abbreviated list. For a more complete listing you can try this site: http://www.mendosa.com/gilistold.htm

Your healthiest form of carbohydrates is from intact grains that have been minimally processed. Foods like whole wheat breads and pasta, brown rice, whole oats, and bulgur wheat. Fruits and vegetables with high fiber content are also excellent. Avoid potatoes, sugar and beverages with added sweetners. Sugars are often disguised by descriptions like high fructose corn syrup, milled cane sugar, evaporated cane juice, dextrose, barley malt syrup, brown rice syrup, molasses, concentrated grape juice. All are highly refined sugars and all have a high Glycemic Index.

Protein
The World Health Organization recommends 0.45 grams of protein per kilogram of your ideal body weight per day. For someone actively training this is increased to 0.8 grams per day and some studies recommend up to 1.6 grams for active athletes and those engaged in serious muscle building activities. Unfortunately the only people in the United States who know exactly how much a gram really is are drug dealers. You can believe it. I travel a great deal in countries that use the metric system and understand that a kilogram is 2.2 pounds. I can approximately visualize how big a pile a half kilogram of meat will make on a sandwich. But, I have no idea of what 4 grams are. To put the protein recommendations into perspective you only have to remember that these numbers translate into

Protein

4 to 12 ounces of meat, fish or chicken. That amount
easily provides the amount of protein suggested.
Indeed, you are also getting protein from many other
foods. Eggs, milk, grains, vegetables and legumes all
contain protein and in Western diets it's hard not to
get enough protein.

Most people in developed countries meet their
daily protein requirements many times over and it is
very unlikely that you need more than you are
already getting no matter how large you want your
muscles to grow or how much exercise you do. High
protein supplements are often advertised to people
doing weight lifting and other intense exercises but
this is thought to be totally unnecessary. Excess protein can be harmful to your health even though the
body breaks it down to be used as energy or stored as

fat. Some studies show large amou its of protein and fat can cause many serious diseases.

It is very unusual to eat pure animal protein. Most come combined with unhealthy stuff like saturated fat. Try to get your protein from skim milk, beans, soy, nuts and whole grains. Fish and skinless chicken are good sources and steer yourself towards lean cuts of meat. Protein from animal sources tend to have a complete set of the 8 (9 for children) amino acids, the building blocks which the body needs to replace and repair muscles, organs and cells. Protein from other sources have only some of these amino acids and vegetarians must be careful to eat a variety of foods to insure they get all 8. Consuming whole grains along with some legumes (beans, peas, lentils) accomplishes this.

Fats
For years I tried to minimize any sort of fat in my diet. I was wrong. The body needs fat to function and what is important is the kind of fat. It's easy to become confused about diet when you start learning about fats. There are saturated fats. These are the "bad" fats and remain solid at room temperatures. They come mainly from animal and dairy products.

Unsaturated fats, the so-called "good fats" are divided into monounsaturated fats and polyunsaturated fats. These come mostly from plant and fish sources. The monounsaturated fats are liquid at room temperatures but may start to solidify in the refrigerator. Polyunsaturated fat is liquid at room and refrigerator temperatures. Unfortunately you also have to worry about trans fats, a man made product, and the

Fat

Omega 3,6,9, components of the unsaturated fats. I'll
try to summarize the fat enigma.

Saturated and unsaturated fats are thought to affect
the cholesterol level in your blood and high cholesterol
has been associated with heart disease. There are two
kinds of cholesterol in your blood. Put simply, low-
density lipoproteins (LDL) clog your arteries and cause
heart attacks. LDL is often referred to as the "bad"
cholesterol. High-density lipoproteins (HDL) clean
out the clogs and are called the "good" cholesterol.

Trans-fats are man-made fats produced by bub-
bling hydrogen through heated liquid fat to making it
solid. Trans-fats are particularly bad because they
raise the LDL and lower the HDL. They have been
outlawed in some cities and most food manufacturers
have removed them from their products. Since label-
ing became mandatory for trans-fats they have pretty
much disappeared from packaged foods. There is no
controversy about trans-fats. They should be totally
eliminated from your diet. They still sneak into your
diet through unlabeled foods. Be careful of pastries
and other stuff with a flaky crust baked by little old
ladies at State Fairs.

Saturated fats which come mainly from meats, sea-
food, whole-milk products, the skin of poultry, egg
yolks and some tropical oils should also be avoided.
They raise both LDL and HDL. Saturated fats and
trans-fats are the "bad" fats. The "good" fats are monounsaturated from olive, canola and peanut oils, most
nuts and avocados, cereals and whole grain wheat.
Fish, cereals, soybean, safflower and cottonseed oils
all provide polyunsaturated fats, which are also good.
The good fats do not seem to have any negative health
effects other than the potential to cause weight gain
since they carry more calories than similar weights of
carbohydrates or protein. Studies also suggest that
you can raise your HDL with vigorous exercise.

Tropical oils, palm and coconut, are saturated fats
and have a negative reputation along with animal and
dairy fats. In the past few years however there has
been some revival of interest by food companies in
using tropical oils to replace the totally discredited

trans-fats. A flurry of studies shows the possibility that tropical fats aren't really that bad. Even so, most nutritionists feel that there are adequate substitutes making it easy to stay away from tropical oils.

Just when you thought it couldn't get any more complicated, nutritionists introduce Omega 3, 6, and 9 fatty acids. These fatty acids are a component of polyunsaturated fats. Omega 3 fatty acids appear to have some very positive health benefits related to heart disease, cancer and even brain functions. Cold-water fish such as salmon, mackerel, sardines and herring contain lots of Omega 3, as do flax seeds, walnuts and grass fed animal products. Farmed salmon, which are grain fed, do not contain as much Omega 3 and the same is true for grain fed beef or eggs from grain fed chickens. Grain fed animals contain much more Omega 6 rather than Omega 3. Some research suggests this change may increase the risk of cancer and heart disease. Omega 9 fatty acids can be manufactured by the body and are not considered nutritionally essential.

Vitamins, Minerals and Supplements
Because of my family's cancer history, when I read about a study showing some vitamin or supplement preventing a kind of cancer it quickly goes into my vitamin cabinet. The cabinet is getting pretty cluttered. Vitamins E and C, Selenium, Turmeric, Resveratol, and CoQ-10 along with all the usual multi-vitamins, calcium, glucosamine-chondroitin, fish and flaxseed oils choke me every morning. I take them all or until the next study proves them worthless. Often these

Norman wondered if the vitamin K would really improve his sex life as much as the ad promised

reversals are only a few months or few years away so I try not to buy the giant economy sizes. While this is a husky handful of pills each morning I fully recognize that 80% of them are doing me no good whatsoever. Worse, I suspect 2 or 3% are positively harmful. The trouble is I don't know which of the remaining 12 or 13% might have some benefit.

It's good insurance to take a multivitamin each day, but taking enormous doses of any vitamin is possibly dangerous. Best, get your vitamins from a varied diet of fresh fruits, vegetables and whole grains. These provide numerous trace and micronutrients that pills can't possible imitate.

Antioxidants are another new discovery to complicate your dilemma on what to eat. These molecules neutralize free radicals. Free radicals are produced by oxidation in your body and can cause cell damage leading to cancers. Some antioxidants are as simple as vitamin C and E. Others have names like zeaxanthin and beta-cryptoxanthin whatever they are. Fortunately even dark chocolate and red wine are thought to have additional antioxidant properties and it's nice to be able to include modest amounts of these in your diet. Rather than go into the ugly details of how this complicated and only partially understood antioxidant process works, just believe the scientists that encourage you to eat lots of colorful and varied fruits and vegetables. Polyphenol antioxidants are nutrients found in colorful fruits and vegetables. These have survived some serious testing and seem to provide health benefits to the immune and cardiovascular system. Nature probably colored bright blueberries, strawberries, peppers, oranges and a host of other foods to catch your attention. Eat them. You'll get lots of antioxidants that'll prevent all sorts of horrible and only partially understood things from happening to your hopefully youthful body.

Water

There is a very simple way to ensure you are drinking enough water. Forget about trying to keep track of how many glasses the latest article suggests you drink every day. Just be sure you are peeing clear. Clear is when your urine is straw color. I for one, being a city guy, am not really certain of the color of straw but I do know that when my pee is yellow it's time to drink lots more water. On one high altitude biking trip (we biked to over 18,000 feet) the guide suggested we drink until we were awakened several times to pee each night. This may have interfered with our sleep but no one had any problems with altitude. Drink lots of water. Notwithstanding a few recent articles on hyponatremia (drinking so much water that it dilutes the sodium in your blood) if you are active it's unlikely you will drink too much.

While bottled water has been all the rage lately, most studies show that tap water is safer. I'd rather be drinking something my local government is testing regularly than paying for a product coming from far away in a plastic bottle.

Balancing Your Nutrients

Different diets and studies recommend quite a large range of carbohydrate-protein-fat ratios. Most sensible nutritionists suggest the following:

Carbohydrates	40 to 60% of your calories
Protein	10 to 15% of your calories
Fat	20 to 30% of your calories

As I said at the beginning of this chapter, theories on diet are constantly changing. Even so I think the latest ideas are honing in on some solid nutritional concepts. Much of the world gets their protein from beans and rice. These people also usually work hard and get lots of exercise. Though they are very poor, by our standards, they don't die from heart attacks and cancer nearly as much as we do eating a rich First World diet. The stuff they do die from, like pneumonia, tuberculosis, parasitic and digestive disease we can usually cure. It probably makes good sense to copy their diets and lifestyles.

In Summary

Eat your veggies.

Choose whole grains over highly processed foods.

Take it easy with red meat and keep your portions of fish and chicken modest.

Be suspicious of all packaged products promising great health benefits.

And, as with exercise—nothing in excess.

6

7 Weight Control

Perhaps I'm lucky or just have a high metabolic rate. I've never had a problem with my weight though I carefully keep it in a very narrow range. Wintertime it creeps up to 162 lbs. and summers, with more bike riding, it goes down to 158 lbs. If it goes over these numbers I kick up the activity a bit and if it falls under I indulge in more dark chocolate or a bit more low-fat ice cream. It's vastly easier to control a small weight gain than trying to lose mega pounds.

Weight Loss or Gain Usually Involves Four Factors

1. *Metabolism*
   Metabolism is how fast your body burns calories. Your resting metabolic rate or basal

Speech bubble: You've met your minimum daily. NOW it's time for JUNK FOOD, JUNK FOOD and more JUNK FOOD!

metabolism is basically a function of genetics and is unlikely to change. Your active metabolic rate is determined by your muscle mass. The more muscles you have, the faster you burn calories. Each pound of muscle, for example, is thought to burn 5 times as many calories as a pound of fat.

2. *Nutrition*
   This is simply your caloric intake. It's what most people think about when dieting. Reducing

caloric intake can lead to loss of weight provided other activities such as exercise stay constant.

3. *Exercise*

   All exercise burns calories. Fast running burns calories quickly. You even burn calories, at a slow rate, while sleeping. The chart on the following page shows a rough approximation of how many calories you burn with different activities. Other things being constant, burning 3,500 calories is usually thought to equal a pound of weight.

4. *Lifestyle*

   Lifestyle is made up of many factors. Do you skip breakfast, snack on junk at lunch and, being "starved", pig out on chicken wings over cocktail hour? Are you constantly traveling and eating at weird hours? Do you consume lots of alcohol? What medications do you take? These will all affect your weight.

It's impossible to change your basic metabolic rate and it may be difficult to vary one's lifestyle. People trying to lose weight must either reduce their caloric intake by dieting or increase their caloric demand by exercising. I like to eat and would rather kick up my activities than skimp on a meal. This is impractical for large weight loses. Nonetheless, a 160 lbs. person will burn about 15 calories a minute by bicycling fast. Since 3,500 calories is generally considered to equal a pound, bike 4 hours over a week and you'll lose a pound. One pound is not a big deal but do this through a 6-month New England biking season, keeping other

Calories Burned per Minute, by Activity at Different Body Weights						
Activity	*Body Weight, lbs.*					
	120	140	160	180	200	220
Bicycling						
10 mph	7	8	9	10	11	12
15 mph	8	9	11	12	14	16
20 mph	13	14	17	18	19	21
25 mph	19	20	21	22	23	24
Running						
10 min/mile	8	10	12	14	16	18
7 min/mile	13	16	18	20	21	23
5 min/mile	16	20	22	24	26	29
Swimming						
30 min/mile	7	9	10	11	12	13
20 min/mile	16	17	18	20	22	23
Skating						
Moderate	5	5	6	7	8	8
Fast	8	10	11	12	14	15
Aerobics	6	7	8	10	11	12
Tennis, singles	6	6	7	8	9	10
Row machine, fast	8	9	11	12	13	15
Jump rope	9	11	12	14	15	17
Martial arts	9	11	12	14	15	17
Cross-country ski	10	12	14	15	17	19

factors equal, and you should lose about 25 pounds. This potential weight loss is negated if you reward yourself with a couple of beers or donuts after each ride.

You can find charts on the Internet that give caloric consumption for almost any activity at different intensity levels. On the opposite page are a few approximate values to give you an idea of calories that you can burn with exercise.

You'll note that calories burned increase with intensity. Double your speed and you double the calories expended. Once again it shows the value of intensity whether you are trying to lose weight or improve your aerobic conditioning.

Don't expect to work yourself furiously one day, burn 3,500 calories and have the scale show a pound loss the next morning. Weight loss from exercise is a cumulative long-term effect. Your body may retain water and make other adjustments to unexpected activity, often disguising any loss. One day I competed in

"Sure enough, this morning's run took off 2 ounces"

an Ironman distance triathlon. I calculated that I burned over 12,000 calories in that race. Rather than lose weight, the scale the next morning showed I gained as my body retained water and dealt with many other physiological stresses from the race.

Raising Your Metabolism

While you cannot raise your resting metabolic rate you may be able to increase it on a temporary basis with exercise. I came upon this idea quite accidentally one day while training for triathlons. Driving to a track to do a hard sprint workout I glanced at my heart rate monitor. I was pleased to see my heart rate in the low 40's even though I was sitting driving a car. Arriving at the track I did an intense workout; a series of mile sprints and my heart rate went to its 90% level, around 140 at that time. After a cool down I drove home and on the way home looked at my heart rate again, curious to see if it returned to the low 40's. To my amazement my heart rate was in the 60's. It remained high for hours. I believe a hard workout increases your metabolic rate and does so for a length of time proportionate to the intensity of the workout. Want to lose weight? Try a run or bike ride before breakfast. My theory is that you'll burn whatever calories you eat at a faster rate.

Diet

Diets are born and fade away almost as quickly as new discount airlines. They help you to lose weight but the real tough part is in keeping the weight off. Since it is almost impossible to always feel hungry, the only satisfactory way to maintain lost weight is to get your caloric intake to equal the consumption level of your activity. You can adjust your calorie intake by portion control and varying the caloric intensity of your foods. A spoonful of fat, for example, has more than double the calories of a spoonful of protein or carbohydrates. Additionally, fruits vegetables and whole grains have lots of fiber in the form of cellulose. The body does not absorb cellulose so it makes you feel full yet adds no calories. Observation of heavy people's eating habits has made me think portion control should be a major part of their diet. We have gone beyond excess with the sizes of our portions in the United States and focusing on controlling these quantities is probably a key factor in a long-term weight control program

Dieting can be hard. Losing weight doesn't have to be. Stay away from cookies, candy, soda, sugar and refined grains. Eat lean meats and forget about fried chicken, bacon, and cheeseburgers. Get lots of fiber that fills you up without adding calories. Forget that French fried potatoes exist and switch to sweet potatoes. Cut the portion size of your protein and increase the whole grains, fruits and vegetables. Eating sensibly and losing weight slowly is a lot safer and easier than crash diets.

Most of all, exercise more.

8 The Lifetime Commitment

As you get older you have to spend more and more time keeping fit. Ultimately you may find yourself spending ALL your time keeping fit. My wife thinks I reached this point years ago. Hopefully by then you'll be retired and have the free hours. Also, hopefully you will be enjoying the exercise enough to find spending all your time working out a positive delight.

Finding the Time and Making Choices

People to whom I describe my philosophy of exercise most often cite lack of time as a reason for skipping or skimping on their workouts. This is more a matter of choices than lack of time. Working people sleep about 8 hours a day and work a similar amount. Meals and commuting take another few hours. Three to

"Sam, I knew your running was going to come in handy some day"

eight hours remain. How you utilize those 3 to 8 hours involves choices. Most Americans, unfortunately, watch 4 or 5 hours of TV each day. You can watch the TV or take a bike ride; visit a friendly neighborhood bar or go for a run; lie on a beach or take a serious swim; chat with friends, play on the Internet or workout. It's your choice. To "die young as late as possible" it's a no-brainer; the choice is working out.

I'm retired. Finding the time for all these workouts is a cinch. But, when I was still working 50 or 60 hours a week my workout schedule wasn't much different. I was seriously competing in triathlons at the time and that involved lots of training. Getting up 30 minutes early provided time for a quick run. Eating at my desk left time for a bike ride or swim at noon. A simple set of weights at home was adequate for strength training. When time is short the intensity of your training is much more important than the duration or even the frequency. A 45-minute bike ride with sprints or hill climbs is vastly more beneficial than a 3-hour slog. Reducing your workouts or missing some of them will have little effect as long as intensity is maintained. Your strength and aerobic conditioning will be unchanged, even over a period of months, if you complete a few intense workouts each week. If you are short of time, trade duration for intensity.

Incorporate workouts into your daily life. Commute by bike, take the stairs rather than the elevator, and walk to nearby shopping instead of driving. Do your own yard-work and snow shoveling. When your car needs servicing toss your bike in the back and ride home rather than seek a ride. Plan active rather than passive vacations. You'll find new places are much more enjoyable viewed from the seat of a bike or on foot than through the window of a car or bus. You can squeeze in workouts early in the morning. Runners are on the streets and gyms are crowded before work every day. My noontime workouts at our company became a communal activity as others at the office joined me. In over 40 years of business I probably didn't have a dozen business lunches. I even got lucky with a major customer at Kellogg's. The buyer was a swimmer. When I called on him at Battle Creek Michigan, rather than go to lunch, we'd swim a mile. Everyone wants to stay young. To do so you have to make a commitment. You will find this commitment is easy to fulfill once you get started and it will bring immediate benefits. Exercise rather than lead a passive life. You will never regret it.

In 1982 after selling a business I wrote a list of 7 rules to guide my life as I started a new company. The rules were mostly business oriented but the one I found myself quoting and remembering most often was Rule 6. Rule 6 was, "Don't let business interfere with your fitness schedule because fitness is life and youth itself and no amount of money will buy that." Believe it—that's sound advice.

Here's an example of a choice I recently decided to make with my diet. After reading *The China Study* I agreed with the author's findings that many health problems, like cancer and heart disease that we experience in the West are due to our diet. We simply eat too many foods rich in animal protein and fats. I decided to cut down on them. This change involved giving up red meat and cutting back drastically on fish, chicken and dairy protein. My wife and sons were surprised knowing how I love my lamb chops, beef ribs, eggs and milk products. But, I found the switch surprisingly simple to live with. It took only a few days to feel comfortable giving up red meat and accomplishing over a 50% reduction in other animal based foods. It was a pleasant switch. You can do the same, fitting exercise and good nutrition into your life so you can lead it as a younger person.

Myths About Aging

I hear lots of baloney from overweight or otherwise unhealthy people justifying their lifestyle. One eminent doctor told me it was healthy to gain weight, as you grow older. Seems he thought it better cushions the body from injuries in falls. Many people continue to warn me about wearing myself out. They prefer to sit around rather than exercise and don't seem to understand that use only makes your body stronger. I've had highly intelligent people use my swim pool and insist that floating or bobbling up and down in the water was every bit as beneficial as swimming laps. Others claim that walking a few miles is equivalent to running that distance. Lazy people will always come up with "brilliant" reasons to stay lazy. You've got to ignore these idiotic conceptions.

"Doesn't anyone just splash around anymore?"

Don't think age will cause a reduction in your athletic capabilities. Researchers at the German Sports University in Cologne analyzed marathon and half marathon times for men and women and found there was little difference in race times for age groups between 20 and 50. For ages 50 to 69 the reduction in performance was only 2% to 4% for each decade. A similar study in International Journal of Sport Medicine mentions declines of 5% per decade for runners in their 50's and 60's.These studies showed that there is little reason to think your fitness will decrease with age. Keep exercising and you will maintain your strength, speed and coordination into your senior years. Those people you see who are creaky and old are the ones who gave up exercise years ago. The few of us who continued to use our bodies find them just as good as when we were young.

Growing older does not have to cause frailty. Frailty is caused by lack of exercise. As you age you lose nerves and each nerve serves one muscle fiber. Loss of these muscle fibers leads to weakening. If you exercise you can increase the size of the remaining muscle fibers and this counteracts the reduction of muscle caused by the loss of nerve fibers. Exercise is the key to maintaining a youthful life style, and finding the time to exercise is the important starting point.

Your bones will weaken if you don't include some sort of high impact or weight training in your program. Running, rope jumping, weightlifting, and any sport that gets you pounding will keep your bone structure strong. Sports like biking and swimming are non-load bearing and must be supplemented with some sort of impact activity. Lazy people think that taking calcium pills will prevent osteoporosis. Calcium supplements can't hurt but it's the stimulation of the bones' structure by exercise that really protects against this disease.

So few people continue to exercise as they age that entering master and senior events at athletic

The real way to die young is to stop aging by no longer having birthdays. This means, of course, that you also have to give up presents and cake and funny little hats. But life is full of ugly trade-offs like that.

competitions is another way to get a great youth inducing ego boost. Categories for older people are available in many sports and if you're at all fit, once you reach 65 or 70, you can be fairly confident of taking home a trophy. I was totally non- athletic as a kid but once I turned 50 I piled up a roomful of triathlon awards. Even if you don't end up on the winner's podium you'll be surprised at how good you'll feel posting finish times better than many youngsters.

Evaluating the Endless Studies

Every week you read or hear about new studies concerning health and diet. Many of them present totally conflicting results. Fiber in your diet prevents bowel cancer. Fiber in your diet has no effect on bowel cancer. Vitamin E reduces the risk of Prostate cancer. Vitamin E has no effect. Estrogen prevents heart attacks. Estrogen causes them.

How to make sense of all this conflicting information that screams at you from the front pages? Here are a few things you should consider.

1. How big was the study and what was its duration?
   Something covering thousands of participants over many years is certainly more valid than one using 6 friends for a weekend.

2. What was being studied?
   Studies on humans are much more believable than those done on animals.

3. What was being measured and is it likely it could be accurately determined?

Blood samples for example would be very objective. How much saturated fat a person ate, unless they were locked in a control room, might be very subjective. It's expensive and difficult to measure people using a controlled environment especially over a long period of time. For this reason most studies rely on questionnaires. But, people's perceptions vary all over the lot. A friend recently diagnosed with breast cancer lamented, "Why did this happen to me? I eat carefully and exercise all the time." This was from someone grossly obese whose only exercise was an occasional slow walk. People's perceptions of their own habits are seldom objective.

4. Who did the study?

Be wary of sensationalism in the news media. Before you believe some exciting new diet or exercise revolution featured in your morning paper consider the above points. Try to learn something about the organization carrying out the study. This is really important. See if they have an economic interest in the results. Studies arriving with a sales pitch and promising great health benefits if you buy some supplement or product are often totally worthless. Not so long ago, remember, cigarette companies had their own studies that claimed there was no proof whatsoever that cigarettes had any negative health risks.

To believe a study it should be carried out by a reputable group and published in a well-known, peer-reviewed journal. Additional studies should back it up. Even then, you can apply the "Bubba" principle. Would your grandmother have believed it?

Sleep

This really isn't part of a lifetime commitment but I didn't know where else to put a few comments on sleep. Sleep is a mysterious process and there doesn't seem to be any consensus on how much sleep you need. Even though sound sleep seems to become more difficult as you age, most sport physiologists, top athletes and coaches suggest at least 8 hours a

As you grow older sleep seems to become more and more difficult

night. You are allowed to take naps to meet this goal. Lots of studies show 7 or 8 hours a night to be ideal though some people argue they can get by on 5 or 6 quite nicely. There is no way to really know except tuning in to what feels best to your own body. If you're not always tired and make adequate fitness gains you're probably getting enough sleep. There is total agreement that exercise improves sleep even if the exercise is done just before bedtime.

Smoking

I never envisioned a smoker buying this book but perhaps a few words are appropriate in the unlikely event some smoker receives it as a gift. Smoking is one of the few activities that have been positively proven to be very detrimental to your health. If you smoke you will die old and sooner. Before you die you will be less healthy and less attractive with more wrinkled skin and an odor repellent to most people. Don't smoke.

Illness and Injury

There have been lots of studies on how fitness affects illness. This is a difficult subject to prove conclusively since there are so many variables, but studies generally show that fit people are healthier. They get fewer colds and less serious diseases. I for one rarely get sick and when I do I recover quickly. The same, I suspect is true with injuries. Younger people certainly heal faster and fit people have many of the characteristics of youth. I recovered very quickly from my recent shoulder operation and while getting physical therapy I observed many patients younger than I but sadly sedentary and overweight. Judging from their exhaustion from the simple exercises they were doing and minimal mobility I can only assume their recovery rate was vastly slower than my own. This is another bonus of staying fit and young. You'll fall ill less often and recover faster when you do.

Never get totally out of shape. Getting back into shape is like dieting to lose lots of weight, painful. Even when injured you can usually find some part of your body that can still exercise. If your legs are in a cast, do upper body weight lifting. After my recent shoulder operation I used my legs while recovering. Two day after I left the operating room I was on an indoor exercise bike. A day later I ran the stadiums at Harvard and within a week biked 100 miles. You don't have to lose your fitness level when confronting injury or other problems. When exercise becomes difficult set some obtainable goals and stick to them.

A Final Benefit

Recent studies suggest that exercise has considerable beneficial affect on your brain as well as your body. Aerobic exercise causes the heart to pump more blood to the brain and this added flow nourishes brain cells. Vigorous exercise seems to make the brain operate more efficiently. A recent study published in the Proceedings of the National Academy of Sciences showed that working out can actually help to grow new brain cells, something previously thought impossible. These

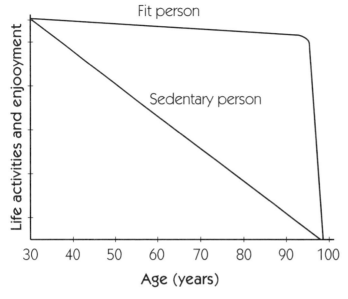

Fit person

Sedentary person

Life activities and enjooyment

30   40   50   60   70   80   90   100

Age (years)

Slow Decline vs Rectangular Life Line

are exciting revelations and research shows that a regular exercise program can stave off some of the mem-
ory loss that comes with aging including Alzheimer's
and other forms of dementia.

Let's face it. Our human death rate is pretty much
100%. We are all going to croak and as my father
used to say "be pushing up daisies" some day. Aging
is often thought a slowly declining line as shown on
the above graph where activities and life enjoyment
decrease as a person ages. But it doesn't have to look
like that. Seek to make your life curve more rectangular. Keep having fun and acting young until the very
end. Not only will your life be more enjoyable but
also the "end" will be as late as possible.